MIRACLE

OF

NAMES

A 500-WORD DESCRIPTION
OF YOUR LIFE AND CHARACTER

BY
CLAYNE CONINGS

Sunstar
PUBLISHING LTD.

Miracle of Names
by Clayne Conings
© United States Copyright, 1996
Sunstar Publishing, Ltd.
116 North Court Street
Fairfield, Iowa 52556

Cover Design: Heather Chicoine

Library of Congress Catalog Card Number: 95-072375
ISBN: 1-887472-03-7

Readers interested in obtaining further information on the
subject matter of this book are invited to correspond with
The Secretary, Sunstar Publishing, Ltd.
116 North Court Street, Fairfield, Iowa 52556
More Sunstar Books:
http://www.newagepage.com

CONTENTS

FOREWORD
by Rodney Charles

Do we have an individual destiny? Of course we do. Our existence proves it and the mind's purpose is to verify the fact. Our different personalities imply a specific destiny or reason. Our happiness and health are entirely dependent on bringing that essence forth. This book may hold the key that will reveal the mystery surrounding your destiny and your name.

You cannot become a member of Destynology, but you can study its concepts. It is a school dedicated to the dissemination of a teaching that has profound implications in the selection of a suitable name.

Destynology differs from conventional Numerology in principle. According to Numerology, all names are good and the qualities of our names represent lessons that each individual must learn. Whereas Destynology, the guiding principle for this book, suggests that without a balanced name, the individual cannot work out the lessons—he will struggle endlessly with his problems and his life will never move beyond this state.

This importance of the correct name is implicit in the Holy Books of Judaism, Buddhism, Hinduism, Christianity and other religious cultures such as the ancient Egyptians and Mayans. In many cultures, baptism and the Name Day are more auspicious than the birthday. Why is this? Unfortunately, over time the meaning has been lost and ceremonies such as baptism have become empty rituals.

The reemergence of this lost knowledge, which the author has called Destynology, allows individuals to choose appropriate names that will give them an advantage in life. With a balanced name, a child will be able to learn more quickly and thus will meet the challenges that lead to mastery of life.

Are we willing to accept the possibility that the proper name can accelerate our progress and move us to greater heights of accomplishment? Without a balanced name, our problems tend to distract us and demand our attention. Our preoccupation with problems may drown us in emotionalism and prevent us from experiencing the beauty of our existence. A strong, intelligent mind does not perceive problems, it deals with the circumstances of life without the influence of emotionalism.

The mind is powerfully affected by language, and the name in particular. An individual with the correct name builds his life on success and is more likely to respond to life's experiences effectively. The underlying concept of names and numbers goes beyond dealing with problems; it elevates the individual to a higher status in life. By studying the concepts of Destynology presented in this book, we give ourselves the knowledge that can change our lives dramatically.

INTRODUCTION

Of those who read the contents of this book, some will find it amusing, others will accept it blindly, and hopefully a few will see its profound implication. The application of the principles involved can truly transform the individual. Few studies of the human psyche can satisfactorily explain why so few people possess the substance of character necessary to deal with the fundamental responsibilities of everyday life, let alone evolve to become a spiritual force.

There are a multitude of theories and courses offered to people who feel inadequate in dealing with aspects of their life, and it is interesting to note that probably less than 3% of these people actually benefit and succeed on the basis of the information given. It is also interesting to note that the few who can deal effectively with the problems of life, such as relationships, the stress of the work place, or finding themselves in satisfactory occupations, never take courses at all. This is because these are not primarily academic problems as much as they are problems of the mind, in terms of the substance and quality of one's character.

An academic education may provide jobs but it has little to do with happiness. This could be demonstrated in a family of several children where perhaps only one of them achieves anything of distinction. Although they may all come from a decent family background, one of them may become a misfit. A moral education may strengthen your character somewhat, but your actual basic character is created through language, your name and an understanding of the principle of a balanced name.

This well-kept secret forms the part of the Kabalah called the Sefer Yetsirah. In Freemasonry the written material dealing with the highest or "thirty-second degree" is referred to as "The Royal Secret" and implies, but does not reveal, an understanding of the ancient mystery concerning the "Lost Word." The Chinese revere numbers, especially the number 8 but have no idea where this superstition originated or what it truly implies. The Mayans of Central America had a history of changing names and a vague sense of its importance, however the knowledge concerning it and the principles involved have been lost to antiquity. In India when you seek to have your fortune told, the first thing the fortuneteller requires is your name and birth date. In the baptismal ceremony of the high English and the Catholic Church the priest asks after giving the child a name, "and what will this name do for you?" After receiving the mysteries of Egypt dealing with the power of numbers in relationship to letters, the Greek Philosopher Pythagoras taught the mysteries and for his efforts his school was burnt to the ground and he and his pupils fled for their lives. The system called numerology has gathered together pieces of this mathematical principle and expanded it into a pseudoscience that has distorted it almost beyond recognition. Numerology seems to be used to satisfy a personal curiosity about oneself and to support a certain vanity. For this reason, serious people looking for truth, along with the academic and scientific community, would not dare to be found looking into books on the subject for fear of ridicule. Through numerology, this work and a very profound principle have been relegated to the scrapheap of occultism.

The great secret here is a principle that deals with equilibrium or the knowledge of how to create a balanced mind. In other words, "Why do a few people possess such an obvious mental advantage over others?

You are your name. You will not consciously exist without a name, nor will you have consciousness if you are not named. When you are asked "Who are you?", you answer by giving your name. You do not point to your body. When you reply to the question "What kind of person are you?", you refer to the invisible qualities that make up your mental characteristics or your personality. The quality of your mind or personality is formed as an individual response to life's experiences as set in motion through language and your name. The human body and its brain cells are designed to respond to the forces of reason or causality.

The function of the human mind is to become aware or gather knowledge about life, not only about things external, but about mind itself—in other words, to become self-conscious. The instinctive species merely respond and carry out their function through a natural consequence of that instinct. As humans we must search through reason before our intuitive (or, could we say, our instinctive) natures reveal a natural rhythm through the process of mental discrimination and truth. This is not done so much through an outward investigation of life but through understanding the mind itself, how it is created, and then how it draws or receives the finer or higher mental impulses through balance and mental development, or a refinement of mind. You could say that consciousness is the essence or reason of life making itself known through human thought and human endeavor.

Consciousness operates through language; language represents the medium through which the invisible element of consciousness makes itself known. In the autobiography of Helen Keller, who was left mute at an early age, she says that until her nurse taught her the rudiments of a language in her teen years, she had absolutely no awareness of anything except the most basic urges. She claims that her life began only when she was introduced to language. So it is with every child who is born and learns a language. In the Christian Holy Book it states "In the beginning was the Word, the Word was with God, and the Word was God." Life literally begins with language. God, the reason of life, requires a vehicle to express and view life and to unfold that which God is. Language holds the key to the expression or unfoldment of consciousness. Language has intelligence simply because the letters or symbols have a mathematical order to them. Change the order of our alphabet, or any alphabet, and you destroy the intelligence and the potential for releasing the forces of consciousness or reason that lie behind the letters or language.

Everything in the universe exists because of a unique mathematical arrangement or relationship of its components. If you could change the relationship of a thing's components, you could change its form. If you rearrange the letters of an alphabet, that alphabet will not take on intelligence and become usable until you establish a mathematical order as a constant.

Why can numbers or mathematics be used to discover the workings or form of all things? What gives them the power of calculation or revelation? It is simply that numbers are arranged in a sequential order: 1 is in the first position, 2 is in the second position and so on. Do not gloss over this idea too quickly. In its simplicity it is quite profound. The shape of the symbol or number is arbitrary, but its position in relation to the other numbers proves its existence and gives it its meaning. We are not merely dealing with a quantitative aspect of a number but an actual quality of a number. After all, it only has quantity and quality because of its position in its sequence or relationship to the other numbers.

The forces of consciousness are actually arranged through the mathematical order of any alphabet and can be understood and observed as they are expressed through the individual who is the name. Your tangible physical body with its brain cells is linked to the conscious forces because you identify yourself through your name. Your true identity is through your name, not your body, although the two are indivisible.

In the same way, sound, like consciousness, is a vibration or wave motion. Sound as a vibration takes form as it strikes our ear drum. Abstract or unmanifest reason, when it is applied to language and becomes an impulse, impinges upon the brain cells and takes form through thought and sensation or consciousness.

In our part of the world, sound is divided into musical tones or a scale to produce many musical variations, all based upon a seven-note system with its semitones to make twelve in all. (The number of notes, of course, is arbitrary.) Consciousness has that same attribute, although it has nine basic qualities with an untold number of variations. In music we are transported into various moods of happiness, sadness or any number of sensations, all through the arrangement or harmonics of the musical tones. A composer hears the music in his mind and must then write it down according to his understanding of the precise mathematical arrangement of notes. Music can be arranged to create discord or harmony depending upon the relationship of one note to the other. The principle is exactly the same when we arrange the forces of consciousness through language and our names. The point here deals with harmony or equilibrium. A balanced name creates a balanced mind.

Self-confidence or positivity, for instance, is either in the name or it is not. If you take a course in positive thinking but positive thinking is not in the name, you will not become positive. People who give these courses know full well that only those who have the attributes of positivity to begin with are the ones who will succeed. The percentage is very small.

In life we can observe extremes in people's personalities. Some have the gift of the gab but can never stop talking long enough to listen to others. On the other hand, there are those who suffer from a lack of this fluid or spontaneous verbal expression. Some people have all the attributes to succeed in business but are absolutely short suited in their ability to deal with domestic responsibilities. There are artists who starve for want of other qualities and scientists who cannot see beyond the limits of their microscope.

Every individual has a function, inclination, or a

sense of something they would like to do, but few ever bring their potential to fruition through their efforts. The spark or current of their life wants expression through action and accomplishment. In a practical sense, if the mind has the substance to deal with the everyday problems of life, there will be harmony. If it cannot, then the frustration will drive the individual to do some strange things.

I am reminded of the gnostic gospel of Thomas, "If you bring forth that which is within you, then that which you bring forth will save you. If you do not bring forth that which is within you, then that which you do not bring forth will destroy you."

All human problems stem from the root cause of an unfulfilled life. We can only bring forth anything through the substance of our mind. We may believe that a past incarnation is responsible for our present misery or that our dysfunctional background is the root cause of our lack of success. These concepts will pull us into a whirlpool, and suck us into the downward spiral of self-pity where there is a perpetual preoccupation with our problematic natures.

The solutions to all problems becomes easier just by balancing your name. If a child has a balanced name from birth, then environment and social influences become secondary to the child's success. The child's own strength and substance of character through that name will eventually propel the youngster to more easily fulfill his natural inclinations.

The following is a demonstration of the powerful influence of your name on your personality, which includes your weaknesses and strengths, your interests, your possible imbalance, and your health. Everything lies revealed in your name.

Throughout our lives we continually ask ourselves the question, "Where am I going?" That question can only be answered when we ask and resolve the question, "WHO AM I?" Self-knowledge, self-awareness, or self-realization all pertain to your perception of what makes you different from every other human being and what gives you your unique purpose in life.

Each human being is unique, with an unlimited potential. All that is required is to awaken the will or the willpower to go forth and accomplish. This "willpower" could be likened to the "passion" that few ever awaken and that drives those few to ever greater achievement. It reminds me of Martin Luther King's pronouncement, "I have a Dream." We hear in his words a "will" or a driving passion, a belief so strong that it allows no fear. In Joseph Campbell's words, he says that each man and woman must find their "bliss." I would say, when spiritual essence within each person begins to express, the power of "will" awakens and the dream is lived. Each person has "free will." Very few ever exercise that freedom. For this we require knowledge and the proper tools. Like a musician, he must know his instrument and his craft thoroughly. After ten or twenty years, if he learns music well and he learns about himself in the process, he may reach the point when he inspires his audience and when they applaud his effort, he bows in humility to his "power." Only then can he truly say "for this was I born!" Now he has his freedom. It is his. He makes no demands.

Every single problem that we encounter through life is related to our direction or lack of direction, and it is ultimately resolved when we understand who we are and where we are going.

Through this work many thousands have changed their names in order to assist themselves in expanding their potential for self-discovery and to bring greater self-confidence into their lives. Each of us who has changed our names would testify to the profound changes that take place. To see a young child growing up who has been given a balanced name at birth, is proof enough of the miracle of this principle. That child will adjust more easily to all life's experiences without trying to escape or rationalize weaknesses. (For any enquiries regarding this work, I refer you to the back of the book for names and addresses.)

The following first names represent the dominant influence in these people's lives. It must be remembered that as you read the analysis of your first name it is only a partial view of your whole personality. This analysis will be shaded by the influences of your surname, the two names combined, as well as your time of birth. You must realize that the impact of the following analysis of your first name only depends upon the fundamental principle of balance between all the influences. The negative or positive influences mentioned in the analyses will actually be intensified or modified according to the overall balance.

To keep things in perspective, I should offer an explanation of all the influences that make up the whole or complete personality. First, there is the time of birth which defines the quality or force of "inclination." This represents the potential only and its degree of expression depends upon the overall balance of the names. With most of us, this inner quality or true path in life is frustrated to some degree. When this occurs, the negative aspect of our nature expresses.

The strongest and most compelling influence is created through the giving of the "first" name. It is this single influence and the following eighty-one analyses that this book deals with. For a complete and comprehensive analysis, all the different aspects of name and birth date must be considered. If anyone cares to further pursue their interest in this work or desires a complete name or life analysis, they can turn to the back of the book for more information.

The last name is not least in influence. It represents the common thread that runs though the life of each member of the family and creates the collective atmosphere in the home. This can be good or bad—

it can be supportive of the individual member or otherwise. As well, it can either add to the strength of the first name or take away from it.

When taken in the proper perspective, you can work out your last name in the same way as the first name (as shown in the back of the book) and read the influence that applies, keeping in mind that the surname is a lesser influence in the total make-up.

Middle names that are not used do not have an influence on the overall character.

If a nickname is used, the amount of influence will be determined by the amount of use.

The combined names, first and last, create what might be termed, the destiny of influence. It is so called because we are compelled to move in a specific direction which may or may not be to our liking.

When we change our names, through marriage or for other reasons, our circumstances definitely change. Our basic character may not seem to change but certain elements in our life are altered, sometimes constructively or otherwise depending again on the principle of a balanced name.

Not only does this principle define human nature, but its power lies in its application to life's problems. In other words, growth or spiritual development is a process that moves us forward only when we can use this knowledge as a reference point for analyzing our challenges in life. Without it we are bound to see our problems as they are colored by our emotions. Our problems exist in our minds. If we cannot accept that idea, we are bound to spend an eternity analyzing the symptomatic elements of each problem without knowing why a problem is a problem in the first place.

To find your name refer to the "Name Directory" at the back of the book (or work out the three-digit number of your name as shown in the next section). If your name is not in the Name Directory and you must work out your three numbers, match them with the appropriate numbers at the heading of one of the following eighty-one analyses. You should note that the numbers at the head of each analysis, beginning with the first one, are arranged sequentially.

WORKING OUT YOUR NAME

```
1  2  3  4  5  6  7  8  9
A  B  C  D  E  F  G  H  I
J  K  L  M  N  O  P  Q  R
S  T  U  V  W  X  Y  Z
```

Looking at the above key chart, you will note that each letter has a numerical equivalent, in that A,J,S have the value of number 1; B,K,T have the value of number 2, and so on.

Now for example, let us work out the name Robert:

```
   6     5
R  O  B  E  R  T
9     2     9  2
```

We begin by making a distinction between the vowels and consonants by placing the numerical value of each vowel above the letter, while we place the numerical value of each consonant below the letter, as shown above.

Now we simply add up the vowels separately, 6+5=11 and then reduce 11 to a single digit by adding 1+1=2. The number 2 then becomes the sum total of the vowels in the name of Robert. We do the same with the consonants. 9+2+9+2=22. Then reducing 22 to a single digit we add 2+2=4. The number 4 becomes the sum total of the consonants. Finally add the total of the vowels (2) plus the total of the consonants (4) equals number 6. It looks like this:

$$
\begin{array}{llll}
6 & 5 & = & 1+1 = 2 \\
R \quad O \quad B \quad E & R \quad T & & \\
9 \quad\quad 2 & 9 \quad 2 & = & 2+2 = 4 \\
\end{array}
$$

then
2+4=6 or 2-4-6

The numerical combination for the name of Robert is a 2-4-6 combination.

Always remember to reduce the totals to a single digit.

Let's try again with the name Harold.

$$
\begin{array}{lll}
1 \quad 6 & & = 7 \\
H \quad A \quad R \quad O \quad L \quad D & & \\
8 \quad 9 \quad\quad 3 \quad 4 & & = (24 = 2+4) = 6 \\
\end{array}
$$

then 7+6 = 4 or 7-6-4

Exception to the rule:

In the name of Lynn for example, where there are no vowels, then the Y becomes the vowel. If the name is spelled Lynne, the Y, of course, becomes a consonant. Only when there are no other vowels in the name does the Y become a vowel.

Beginning on page 269, find your name in the alphabetical list and the corresponding three numbers that are at the end of your name. These three numbers should be identical to the three numbers at the beginning of your analysis. To help locate the correct analysis, you should note that the the three-number formulas are arranged in sequential order.

1-1-2

Walt Max Ann Larry Bernice Nan Marilyn Craig Joshua Shawn Christina Tristan Evelyn Nina Denise Christian April

This is a complex personality in that it desires to be independent and self-sufficient but invariably ends up being accommodating and a little passive. These people have a great desire to speak their minds yet are compelled to be nice. This ultimately produces conversation that is safe and not too deep. They are sociable and friendly when they have to be but are relieved when they can get away by themselves.

Only they will realize the conflict of this dual influence. On the one hand, they are always struggling to achieve a sense of their own worth in their attempt to be their own boss, and yet they cannot quite push themselves to the top. Working for others in a subordinate role is always a source of frustration. While they are very easy to get along with because of their pleasing nature, they resent being taken advantage of. It is difficult for them to say no, for fear of disappointing others.

They are seldom understood and acknowledged

for their deeper thoughts because of their accommodating natures. When they do get a chance to express
their personal views, they are aware that they have not
been understood. Their verbal expression can flow
easily at times but in the company of the more intellectual types they can become tongue-tied, frustrated
or they just acquiesce. In their day-to-day manner
they are pleasing and friendly. Because of their caring
natures, people are drawn to them. Only later do we
see the independent side of their natures. This is a
quality that can be self-effacing. For this reason they
must be careful not to become lazy and procrastinating.

They function best when they have room to move
and create without the interference of others. They
soon learn that they require their own space with
only a certain amount of contact with others. This
contrasting influence produces a fluctuation of
feeling, from the need for freedom on one hand to a
desire for understanding and affection on the other.
It can be difficult for them to reconcile these two
opposite influences without experiencing a certain
amount of frustration.

While in their independent mode they can be
quite creative in working with their hands. It is this
creative aspect of their personality that is the
strongest. The social side of their nature is at times a
little superficial. They mostly need to cultivate their
creative potential away from people, otherwise this

conflict of qualities will cause them to lose interest in life. The consequence of this will affect their concentration and their motivation and could cause them to become somewhat indulgent in their appetites.

They must exercise discipline if they are to express their potential in creativity. Their weakness lies in the senses of the head as well as their kidneys.

1-2-3

Marg Martin Rita Ellen Nellie Mary Cathy Nancy May Jeffrey Lindsay Amy Esther

These people possess the qualities of independence, self-expression and a carefree attitude towards life. Their desire is to be free from monotony and any kind of work that is tedious and routine. Being independent, they have a great need to work and function without the interference of others. They need to sing and dance their way through life.

Even though this is a fairly emotional and inspirational quality, they will find difficulty in drawing from deep within themselves. This lack of depth will curtail their musical and artistic expression to some degree. While true artists abandon themselves in an outward display of emotional and artistic expression, these people will tend to fall short of being able to completely let go. Consequently, they will feel frustrated and a bit wooden when called upon to draw from the depths of their feelings.

Even in conversation they grasp for words to explain themselves but it is usually in vain. Because of their intellectual shortcomings, they soon learn to take life less seriously than others. They are playful and spontaneous with a desire to see and make people happy. In discussion, they tend to measure others' ideas a little too much from a "self" standard, and therefore, find that a friendly debate can quickly turn into an argument. They do not make good listeners. The urge for self-expression overcomes the need to be silent and to intuit or feel the other person's needs and feelings. They could be accused of being stubborn and resistant to the ideas of others.

This strong "self" orientation is best expressed as a form of self-projection or creativity where their actions are not answerable to others. They must have an environment where they are free to allow their personal creativity to open up to originality of thought.

If they are naturally sociable, as calculated through their time of birth, and find a need for deeper contact with others, they will always be found wanting because it is difficult for them to grasp the more abstract and philosophical ideas of the intellectual and theoretical mind.

In their own social circles, they are loyal, happy and helpful types. Organization and detail are not their strong points, and they must learn to finish the things they start. While they have an ear for music and dance, they must learn discipline or they will never perfect anything. If they do not pursue an artistic outlet, then life can become a drudgery and the negative side of their character will express itself through intolerance and criticism of others.

They like nothing better than to see others happy. They are quite strong and positive in their outlook and generally keep themselves fit and healthy. Moods and depression are not part of their nature. Giving to others comes easy for them. Their love and generosity keep them vibrant and eternally optimistic.

Their weakness lies in the senses of the head, in the skin, and the extremities (hands and feet).

1-3-4

David Lee Al Jessie Wilma Daisy Ryan Alvin Danny Jeremy Gina Kyla Linda Tracy Ali Jabir Elspeth Inga

Here we have people with one-track minds who are hard working, reliable, persevering and a wee bit stubborn. Nothing daunts them once they are on the right track. They are not particularly flexible. They will only change their position or viewpoint when they can prove it satisfactorily in their own mind through their own experience. Theirs is the lesson of scientific enquiry and proof.

They have patience and a keen mind for detail and enter into their interests with a mental scrutiny and an eye for logic. It is usually the practical fields of mathematics, computers, mechanics, accounting, or anything that pertains to the five senses that attracts their interest. Books of nonfiction and philosophical theory leave them high and dry unless they can approach them with the tools of science.

As children they are difficult to discipline because of their headstrong manner and their need to discover for themselves. They can generally only accept that which comes within the realm of their own experience. Therefore their measurement of other's thoughts and ideas is always to their own experiences and this can make it difficult for them in close association. They can be unbendable.

They are capable of hard work and long hours with an enormous capacity for endurance. Their loyalty and steadfastness make them reliable employees. If they are in positions of leadership, they can be hard taskmasters and insensitive to the softer types.

Because of their strong level of independence, they must do things in their own way. This quality does not lend itself to easy relationships in marriage because their ability to listen is hampered by their own strong viewpoints.

When they are focused on their work or hobbies, they possess a great capacity for concentration and an ability to finish what they start. They can stay in a trade or profession their entire working life without desiring any change and be quite happy. Because of this persevering quality, they can accomplish a great deal in whatever field they are interested in.

It is this penchant for detail that gives them their interest in science and the world of form and fact. They marvel at how things work and love to tinker and take things apart and they know exactly how to put a thing back together again.

While these names have many fine qualities, their drawback is their inability to see and appreciate the vastness of life. They can, therefore, become lost in the details of form and fail to go beyond that which encompasses the five senses. This is the typical quality that sees science as the means of answering all questions pertaining to life. They can be a little too materialistic.

Any tension they would suffer would affect them through the stomach and intestinal tract. Constipation and its effects are their main health problem, as well as being affected through the senses of the head.

1-4-5

Frank Kenneth Ethel Irma Lisa Ida Clay Marvin Caitlin Carly Chelsey Shelley Stacy Vivian Eve Ravi Lars

Hard-nosed, independent and difficult to discipline are the main characteristics of these people. They will find their own way in life without anybody's help. They are strong-willed and stubborn. This may be an asset in being able to achieve their personal ambitions, but is a liability in their relationships with people.

In their conversation they are direct and honest but may lack the ability to see another's point of view because of a tendency to judge exclusively from their own experience. They can become fighting-mad when they are opposed or challenged for their stand on issues concerning points of principle. Their reactive natures can be a source of trouble because of their quickness to judge.

These people are hard working and reliable as long as they are left alone. They are restless and ambitious and must not be confined in any way. Their creative natures will develop only when they have found their own activity and are able to develop their originality free from the interference of others.

Because of their basic antisocial natures, they will

suffer an intolerable frustration if their true natures are innately social as determined through the time of their birth.

If there is some degree of balance between their inner and outer natures, then there is nothing to stop them from reaching their goals, although even then they will wonder why getting along with others is so difficult.

This is a quality that possesses stamina, perseverance and a lot of determination. If they are repressed in any way, this powerful force will turn against itself or others and can be quite destructive. They are quite physical and require outlets that challenge their physical prowess.

This is not generally an intellectual or a naturally refined quality, and consequently these people will find themselves out of place in an environment of gentility or where the conversation deals with abstractions or philosophical theory. Their verbal expression is more candid or even blunt. They do not have the verbal fluidity of some. Sometimes their awkwardness can be vented through sarcasm and intolerance of others' views. Their major setbacks in life stem from their "self-measurement" of others' ideas. They can be too quick to respond to others' thoughts without giving them due consideration. Others may find them disruptive and impossible to engage in meaningful conversation. They are loyal and true to the few friends they have.

They are pioneers when pursuing their interests and always require change and excitement or boredom can set in very quickly.

Truth and justice can become powerful motivators in their life. They will stop at nothing to see justice done, but they must guard against being motivated by anger or they will become blind to their noble purpose.

This is a quality that is usually quite healthy if they have a physical outlet for their energy, otherwise they will suffer head tension affecting the senses of the head. They are also prone to stomach upsets and ulcers.

1-5-6

Gary Sam Karl Irene Sally Darcy Elke Stephen Blair Bryan Darryl Grant Ian Lydia Hans

These people have good sense, responsibility and strong opinions. They are not afraid of speaking out but must learn the value of discretion and keeping good counsel. It is their candid manner of speaking that offends, even though it comes from a place of honesty and is sincere. They have the intelligence to hold back but at times their blunt manner, being a natural part of their character, will offend despite their intentions. In consequence they could withhold their thoughts for fear of upsetting others.

There is integrity and concern for others in this influence. Sometimes their strong sense of responsibility and what they think is right or wrong can cause them to become overbearing and interfering. They want the best for their children but must learn to stand back a little and watch them from a distance, without too much instruction.

This quality is not deeply intellectual and suffers from the problem of "self-measurement." Individual experience, in other words, becomes the basis from which they draw their conclusions. There is little sensitivity to intuit another person's thoughts and feelings. While their response is honest and often quite sensible, it is still from their own point of view and not a conscious response from knowing the deep intention of another person. They are very independent, which becomes an asset and a liability. It is their strength because it provides self-initiative and confidence. It is a problem when it is not balanced with the skills of communication. Their verbal communication is not very fluid or reciprocal when there is a lack of depth and sensitivity.

Having said these things, these people are generally quite successful because they are hard working and reliable. They need to be in a position where they can work independently, free from the interference of others. Their self-initiative allows them to work upward quickly because they are not afraid, and they want to help. They are only happy when they are in charge and when their ideas are accepted and not challenged. Unfortunately they can be "straw bosses" without the qualities that make for good leadership. They thrive best in their own businesses. Their common sense allows them to make good decisions. They are fair and just in their dealings.

In relationships they are loyal and committed to working things out, but there is a strong tendency to want things their own way. This inflexibility is not easy on working partnerships or in marriages. Again, it could be said that they hear you but they are not listening. They make good mothers and fathers because of a natural maternal or paternal instinct. It is in their hearts to do the right thing for their children and their community. This conflict between the urge to serve others and the need for compliance represents the area of their life which is their perpetual challenge. This awkward trait can unnerve them as they tread through life or they push their way through obstacles and gain the reputation of being too bossy.

Tension will affect them through the senses of the head.

1-6-7

Jack Harry Carl Sylvia Hilda Bette Richard Brad Calvin Derek Francis William Mark Kathryn Hilma Basil Hank Neville

This is your typical "lone wolf" who prefers the out-of-doors where nature and the elements provide the basis for relaxation and contemplation. They are compelled by this quality to seek their happiness alone and isolated. Independence is their strong point and sometimes their weakness. Their great creativity is only awakened when they are alone and quiet. Theirs is the pioneering spirit which seeks expression through originality.

These people can suffer a great deal of frustration if their date of birth inclines them in any way towards a social life, and where they are called upon to express themselves verbally.

They do not relate well to people or to crowds. They express themselves candidly or even bluntly without ever meaning offense. Theirs is a life of misunderstanding and loneliness, particularly if they are innately social. They can never quite find the right words to express their feelings and deeper sentiments.

This is a quality that requires a physical outlet for

their energies. They are not good at debate and would feel awkward among the more intellectual types. Their perspective is either black or white and they will let you know point blank exactly how they feel. They could express themselves through writing or any avenue where they are left alone to do it their way.

Honesty, reliability and loyalty are the keynotes of these people. They are not afraid of hard work; endurance and physical stamina will see them through their projects.

Due to their lack of social graces, they can be forced to seek a life of seclusion. It is very difficult for them to support others in their thoughts as they do not have the capacity to listen without measuring from a "self" standard. Their verbal expression is usually restricted to thoughts pertaining to their own life, or they remain silent and uninterested in joining the discussion.

This quality ultimately leads to a more reclusive life as they learn to accept their social shortcomings. When they are frustrated from want of the right words and spontaneous expression, they can be caustic and blunt and never know how to show affection and warmth. It is very difficult for them to show or express the little gestures of kindness or refinements that form the basis for enduring relationships.

On the other hand, their loyalty and integrity make them true friends even though they may be incapable of showing love openly.

Their perseverance allows them to see things through. If they do not suffer from the stigma of a dual nature that is inwardly social and outwardly anti-social, then they could be quite accomplished in almost anything they put their mind to that does not require diplomacy and tact.

They have a headstrong nature that is both an asset and a liability. Unfortunately it does not lend itself easily to loving relationships.

They have a rugged nature that loves nature. This is their escape from the noise and confusion of the marketplace.

Their weakness lies in the senses of the head as well as the heart, lungs and bronchial organs.

1-7-8

Andy Ray Helen Steve Virginia Randy Gavin Leslie Spencer Wesley Crystal Tina Faith Cynthia Brian Pierre

Here we have a strong masculine force, confident, outspoken, and a little bit insensitive to the feelings of others. Ambition and drive can move these people up the corporate ladder, but they must be careful of their candid way of speaking to others. This could be their nemesis. They have a strong desire to be in their own business. They are good organizers, hard workers and demanding bosses. As housewives they usually have control of the purse strings. Their biggest problem is their lack of diplomacy.

This is a very independent quality. In childhood it isn't long before they are off on their own. Because they do not work well with others, they seek to create situations where they are in control and their authority is not questioned. This of course does not bode well in relationships. This is not an easy quality to live with because, on one hand, they have initiative and the force of their personality to drive them, but on the other hand, pity the poor person who gets in their way.

This is a strong physical force with endurance and

stamina. They love to pit themselves against nature or against their opponents in sports.

They are honest and not afraid to speak their minds. They could easily offend the more sensitive types but it is not usually intentional. These people are hard, loyal workers when left alone to do things in their own way. They have their strong opinions and base them on their own experiences exclusively. As friends they will never let you down.

Their ambition is usually directed toward business and finance with the goal of becoming financially independent. They have to watch that they do not become entirely materialistic.

They are not naturally philosophical and can be skeptical about anything that is too theoretical. Because of their limitation in speech, they will let you know how they see things, and it does not particularly encourage further conversation.

Their measurement of life and other's thoughts is purely from the basis of their own experiences, and this makes conversation with them quite difficult at times. They can never quite find the right words to express their thoughts, and this can be a source of great frustration. For this reason they end up blurting things out with the force of their frustration.

Since nothing daunts them, they can persevere and succeed as long as they do not have to deal with the problems of people. They are just and fair in their dealings, with a shrewd eye for making a dollar.

This quality is difficult on a woman because it tends to make her a little bit hard, which invariably affects her relationships with men and leads her to believe that she can do without them, particularly in marriage. She is quite capable of managing her own affairs.

These are not easy names for people who are basically inspirational by right of their birth date.

Head tension and problems related to the generative organs are their weakness when there is too much imbalance. Women can also suffer problems in childbirth.

1-8-9

Debbie Stan Jennifer Ernest Patsy Matt Eddie Garth Jay Sandy Tammy Deirdre Dinah Miriam Salim Yasmin

Two strong urges govern the lives of these people: to work or function independently without any interference from others and the driving urge to find love. The first is a possibility if the rest of the name is balanced. The second is very unlikely. In combination these two aspects are not easy to reconcile. In relationships there is often a difficulty because the first requirement is the need to be free from any imposing threat to their independence. While on the other hand their need for love, being as strong as it is, is often repulsed in the ensuing conflict between the need for love and the need for independence.

These people are headstrong and forceful. They are determined and have the power and perseverance to go after their objectives and to work hard. Even though they need the loving association of people, they are not easy to work for or with. Their tempers easily flare up and their candid manner of expression is not easy to take. They will fight to govern their temper for an eternity. It can be aroused on an impulse or the slightest provocation. When life is going along quite nicely their loving natures can express in gestures of kindness and generosity, but these moments are usually short-lived. They have the ability to put their best foot forward when required and their charm can be quite disarming.

The emotional aspect of their natures must have an outlet through art and other creative avenues. They have a tremendous potential for a unique and original expression of their talents. If their lives are frustrated and their creativity is suppressed, they can become quite emotionally indulgent.

Because their basic nature through the name is physical, the love aspect, when aroused, invariably moves to the emotional and physical regions. The need for love expression is quite strong with these types but, because of the strong physical orientation, enduring and growing relationships become quite difficult. Initially, when falling in love, they can give a lot to the relationship but their strong self-orientation eventually breaks it down. They cannot easily master the requirement of "give and take." Even then, love is foremost on their minds, always looking for it in everyone they meet. Hopefully, through their disappointment in love, they will regard it with an eye to its universal and spiritual side.

In little ways they can be kind and very giving souls, considerate and warm, passionate and compassionate. They are moved to work for a greater and humanitarian purpose. Their strong measurement of other's faults from a "self" standard is their downfall in their personal relationships.

When left alone to work on their own initiative, they are reliable and innovative. They are loyal and dependable when their freedom is not curtailed. These names do not produce a depth of mind. Their lack of intellectual development make them quite skeptical of philosophical theories. They are not good listeners.

Their weakness lies in the senses of the head and the nervous system.

1-9-1

Peter Ralph Dan Pat Kay Barry Hilary Ivan Brittany Gillian Kimberley Alf Dina Nadir Meredith

These people, unlike the soft impressionable types, are independent, strong willed, and even stubborn at times. This is a quality that requires its own space in order to function as a creative force, independent and free of any interference from others. As children they can be difficult to manage and discipline because of their headstrong manner. They move towards independence early in life and strive to strike out on their own as soon as they possibly can.

This is a completely honest quality, dependable, and up front in everything they do and say. In their speech they are candid, and sometimes even blunt to the point that they can offend others, but not intentionally. They have an ingenuity in figuring things out if left alone to do so. Theirs is the quality of originality.

They have the perseverance and endurance to push through any obstacles that might try to stop them, and so they achieve almost anything that they put their minds to. In one sense they are appreciated by others because of their open and honest ways of dealing with them, but they lack in the social graces and often fall short of the required diplomacy in certain situations. They can, in fact, feel out of place in the company of the more sophisticated and intellectual types. They would feel awkward and out of place in debates and where they need to listen carefully to another's point of view.

These people are more physically active types who do not like to spend a lot of time talking about things. Their weakness in not being able to understand or see clearly another's point of view makes it difficult for them to relate deeply in the more intimate matters of love and marriage.

Through life, as they discover that they have difficulty relating well in relationships, there is a tendency to become more and more independent to the point of becoming somewhat antisocial. They are a little too self-oriented, and may lack what is needed to function well with people on the deeper levels of communication.

Their physical weakness lies in the senses of the head, through problems affecting them in the eyes, ears, teeth, sinuses or through loss of hair. If they have injuries it is usually to their extremities—the hands, head, or feet.

This is a positive and confident quality that thrives on initiative when focused on their own projects.

2-1-3

Rose Anna Owen Ronnie Leroy Sandra Joe Graham Sara Charlene Marshall Royce Sasha Jocelyn Bianca Geraldine Simone

As children these people are happy, energetic, playful, and loving. They love to tease and have fun and never take life too seriously, and this character trait carries on throughout their lives. They have the gift of the gab and, at times, they can get carried away with it. They are artistic and creative but quite scattered in their efforts and seldom finish the things they start. They are warm, friendly, and outgoing to everyone and are strongly drawn to the opposite sex.

This is a soft, loving and impressionable quality, that requires encouragement, support, and a strong helping hand if they are to have any degree of success in their lives. Lacking in self-discipline, they must be careful that they are not influenced and drawn into association with those who would mislead them. When disciplined into such fields as dancing, music, or public speaking they can excel. They make fine entertainers.

If they find themselves doing mundane or routine

types of work, they become restless, unhappy and unreliable workers. This is a quality that is not suited to heavy physical labor, or to anything that requires hard work or a focus on detail. They have a sensitivity to the feelings of others and work best in association with others, where they can help and interact on a fun and happy level.

Being emotional types, they thrive on and are motivated through inspiration, but due to a lack of concentration and staying power, they most often fail to persevere in their endeavor. In their interaction with others, their accommodating natures allow them to flow into conversation with almost anyone. Their speech is so fluid that at times they can hardly stop it. Being social types they must be careful about their conversations regarding other people. This is not a deep or philosophical influence.

This is an affectionate, intuitive, and feeling quality that depends on and works well with others. Lacking independence and individuality, these people need the proper direction and guidance if they are to succeed in life. If they are not disciplined and directed into artistic fields, they can become indulgent in their physical appetites. Their creative potential knows no bounds, but if misdirected they can become lazy, and influenced by life in the fast lane.

Physically, they are susceptible to problems affecting them in the kidneys, liver, or the blood stream. They must learn to stay away from too many sweet foods or they can be affected through diabetes and other blood diseases. They are also prone to poor circulation, and swollen ankles later on in life.

2-2-4

Allan Joyce Josie Nathan Christopher Graeme Tara Kathleen Nicole Theresa Maya Chandra

In a world that requires so much paperwork, research, and attention to detail, it is these people who find themselves compelled to carry out those tasks that are often thankless.

They have a naturally friendly and accommodating nature with a mind for detail and a capacity for the mundane tasks that nobody else wants to do. If their inner nature, through their birth date, is contrary or, should we say, inspirational, then they would be compelled into the mundane against their true desire. These names lack the confidence to strike out on their own, therefore they invariably end up working for others in positions that usually do not lead anywhere. Their lack of initiative will keep them from getting ahead in life.

The one way they could progress is by utilizing their natural ability to deal with details. This could be applied to study and education. They have an aptitude for research, accounting, or anything that requires attention to detail but they do not want to get their hands dirty.

This is not a naturally deep or ambitious influence and they must strive hard to cultivate a deeper side or perpetually find themselves working at tasks that are uninteresting and time consuming. Literally or figuratively speaking, their lives can be spent picking up after others. It is interesting that while they are compelled into the mundane, they well know they would rather be doing something else more interesting.

They have an openness and a warmth with a great love for people. Their pleasant personalities make them good hosts or hostesses. They can make you feel welcome and relaxed but must guard against becoming involved in conversation that is mostly small talk. Their aim is to please and avoid any possibility of embarrassment, so keeping the conversation simple is the best policy.

They have a capacity for intellectual development along practical lines if the rest of their make-up allows for its development. If not, then their skepticism and lack of drive keeps them perpetually stuck in the mundane. It is this interesting mental dichotomy of their name influence that could promote intellectual activity but usually expresses through satisfying the urge to talk about people.

When they do get down to working at their personal projects, they can work diligently and patiently for hours. They have concentration and the ability to stick to their tasks.

While they have the potential to apply discipline at

work when it is absolutely necessary, they find it quite difficult to discipline their appetites. It is imperative that they eat properly and exercise, otherwise their health will suffer. They are not naturally interested in physical activity and tend to indulge in foods that are not good for them. If this happens, they will suffer in the stomach and intestinal tract, particularly through constipation. They are also prone to problems affecting the fluid functions as well as the kidneys. They require a great deal of rest.

2-3-5

Leo Yvonne Errol Earle Lara Bonnie Sheldon Patricia Marlene Darlene Chantal Cara Gregory Melanie Harriette Kayla

These people are quick-minded, clever, critical, and impulsive. In these names we have two qualities that are sometimes difficult to reconcile. First of all, they crave understanding and require the nurturing element found in friendships. They have the ability to put their best foot forward when necessary but suffer a short fuse when it comes to tolerating fools because this other element in their dual nature reacts very quickly to injustice, or when they themselves are criticized.

Sometimes they are very sociable, while at other times they find people somewhat intolerable. They are very quick to react and often without consideration of other's feelings. Because of this impulsive tendency they may suffer moments of regret at their outbursts of temper.

If the rest of their make-up provides some balance, they can be exceedingly creative, but if they are thwarted, they can become quite depressed and hard on themselves and others. They can be loyal supporters when they are on your side and fierce opponents when fighting for a cause.

If their soft sociable side predominates, then their consideration of others is foremost in their minds; only when pushed against a wall will they come out fighting. These people need a challenge otherwise life becomes dull and boring. For this reason, they must guard against being influenced by others and consequently drawn into the wrong crowds. They are impressionable and not past taking a chance just to have an experience.

If this dynamic and creative force is directed toward a constructive endeavor, they can be extremely creative. At times they can be fearless in their attempts to discover a truth or when pursuing a personal challenge. Fighting for the underdog and supporting a just cause is where they could shine.

Their restless nature sees them always seeking new ideas and adventures. When anything becomes too routine, further fields always look greener. Their life could be a series of misadventures or projects uncompleted. They pick things up very quickly, but as soon as they have discovered how something works, boredom sets in and they are off to something new. They can become quite learned about many things but still unsettled in their lives. If their work satisfies the need for variety, challenge, and a level of independence, then they could find a level of fulfillment.

Relationships are not always easy for them because

of their impulsiveness, particularly if they have no avenue or outlet for their great creativity. One side of their dual nature needs to understand the lesson of merging with others, while the other side requires freedom and independence. This is why these people find long-term relationships difficult.

When they are repressed they can suffer from nervous exhaustion or mental breakdowns. In their physical health they are prone to weak kidneys and stomach upsets.

2-4-6

Robert Hector Connie Maria Joel Isaac Alisa Camilla Maia Devon Leanne Fabian Matilda Rashida Larisa

Soft, intelligent, responsible, but a little lacking in confidence are the main qualities of these people. They can get ahead in life but in supportive roles or with academic credentials that allow them to become professionals working under the banner of an institution. If they choose to go into business, it is in partnership with others. This is a social influence that desires the company of people and works well with them. They are accommodating and perceptive of other's needs.

This easygoing and gentle influence adapts itself to a less harsh or competitive environment. They do not like to get their hands dirty. Diplomacy and tact are their means of getting ahead. They sense a person's discomfort and will do what is necessary to make them feel easy. Pleasing others comes naturally. Their caring and responsible natures move quickly to assist others whenever possible. Their maternal or paternal quality makes them good teachers and parents. They take their responsibilities quite seriously.

Their minds are clear and perceptive and they possess an analytical ability. They can take things quite seriously and tend to worry a little too much at times. This preoccupation with worry can lead to procrastination, as a way of dealing with nagging problems. If there is too much pressure in their lives, they could succumb through loss of confidence and ultimately become a little lazy. They feel more comfortable and supported in association with the opposite sex. Normally this is quite a nice quality except that they lack self-initiative. They are buoyed up when they are in association with others, but lack the strength when a situation calls them to act with force and self-determination.

At times they can be quite decisive and at other times they vacillate. The ability to confront issues is difficult. This is because they are so aware and affected by people's feelings and their own involvement that it seems better to avoid the situation rather than suffer any embarrassment. In their highest sense, if they could conceive of a way of solving a dispute or altercation amicably, they would certainly do it. Unfortunately they will fluctuate in their decision to resolve an issue.

They need to be in positions of responsibility where they are recognized as an authority. It is their knowledge, not their leadership ability that is admired. They may not have quite the strength to become an effective leader, and yet there would be the desire to be recognized as one. While there is an astuteness of mind here, they could fail to gain the recognition that they think they deserve. They may not have quite the push necessary to reach the heights of personal accomplishment.

As an intellectual force they can hold their own. They are practical with a great deal of common sense. This is a social force, not a physical one, so they must not forget to get sufficient exercise if they desire to stay healthy. Their appetites lean towards the sweet foods and any indulgence in them will affect their kidneys and pancreas.

2-5-7

Martha Nelson Clarence Elizabeth Marisa Adrienne Stephanie Trenton Tyrone Chloe Karla Talia Sheena Annette Wanda Arran

These names produce a super-sensitive condition that is not of this world. This world is too harsh, crass and competitive for these types. Their reaction to the noise and confusion of the busy marketplace awakens the urge to escape into the quiet of nature or the seclusion they find in their own privacy. They need plenty of time to themselves. This private time should be spent reading or writing and contemplating the deeper and more meaningful aspects of life. They are poets and romantics by nature.

Their idealism needs to be expressed among their own kind, which they seldom, if ever, find. Being unable to find people who understand their deep feelings, they generally go inward and soon learn to keep their thoughts to themselves. From early childhood they begin to feel, if only unconsciously, that nobody understands them. In fact they do not even understand themselves or their changing moods which are difficult to control.

If the world wasn't so fierce and aggressive, these people could develop their natural skills as dreamers or idealists providing mankind with a vision of peace, refinement and beauty. As it is, they retreat into themselves and suffer the consequences of working environments that rob them of their peace of mind. If the rest of their mental make-up drives them into the normal work-a-day world, then they can become difficult to work with because of their changing moods.

They are so sensitive that at times they can be psychic, picking up feelings and thoughts from others and being affected by any form of discord in their environment. This is particularly so if they have no natural outlet through writing or other refined art forms. At times their thoughts can be quite disturbing.

There is a mystical quality in these names that draws them to religious studies or the occult. They should be careful not to become drawn into mysticism wherein lie theories and ideas that pull them into realms of unreality. When this happens they dream and speculate about fantastic stories that have no basis in reality and that keep them in a kind of trance. They should realize that idealism is useless if it cannot be applied to some specific and practical action.

They are artists who are inspired by beauty. Their souls crave for affection and love. They have a deep side to their nature that invariably gets covered up by their spontaneous and accommodating natures. They would never consider hurting anything or anyone. Because they are so acquiescent, they tend to lose their individuality and, over a period of time, they can lose their depth and become shallow minds seeking people purely for the comfort and association that they crave so much.

They have an innocent beauty and charm, but if their minds are not cultivated along artistic and philosophical lines, they become shy and introverted, going along with things without meaning or purpose.

They are usually too sensitive to be disciplined and healthy, and succumb to diseases affecting the heart, lungs and bronchial organs as well as the fluid functions.

2-6-8

Trevor Clara Isobel Cleo Carla Serena Jana Cole Preston Randall Alicia Chelsea Danielle

Sociability and ambition along financial lines represent the main attributes of these names. It is through people that they move forward in life. They rely on people far more than they are likely to admit. While they can be successful, it is not through the sweat of their own brows. They possess charm and a certain gentility but could be accused of being social climbers.

This is quite a nice influence. Intelligence, poise and diplomacy give nice aspects to their character. Their deficiency could be a lack of self-initiative and feeling for spiritual truths or a deeper and more philosophical feeling for life. It is through the support of others that they gain their strength. Perhaps it could be said that others benefit by the supportive influence of these types. They are perfect hosts who make you feel welcome and at ease.

Here we have an ambition that is directed toward material pursuits. They have refinement and rich tastes and an eye for color, harmony, and a balanced decor. Their homes and their clothes demonstrate their material values. Everything is the best that they can afford, and perhaps a little showy.

They are career-minded and can work well when using their social and organizational skills. In a business environment, their soft way and their natural ability to organize make them good managers and supervisors. They have a insight into people and their intentions and are not easily swayed by emotion. Their minds allow them to reason with a certain degree of dispassionate objectivity.

Because of this soft, easygoing quality, there is a desire for an easy life without too much hard work. They work for security and financial independence. It is through investments and financial planning that they work to secure their future. This is not a profound or deep philosophical influence and, therefore, their futures are considered and secured from a material standpoint, rather than from a creative one. From a spiritual point of view, our future can really only be guaranteed from the basis of our spiritual, mental or creative development. These people cannot easily grasp the deeper aspects of life beyond materiality.

These people may have a wealth complex and the woman desires to marry into wealth.

Their outward propriety can sometimes belie their soft affectionate nature. They are romantics at heart and dreamers but always with an eye towards how to make a dollar.

They have a way with words and a charm that can get them what they want and where they want to go. If they were to find themselves having to depend on their own initiative, they would discover their lack of self-reliance. They are not independent types and this could eventually cause them to become too dependent on others.

They make conversation easily and are good listeners. They are trendy and conform to all the socially accepted concepts of the day. Their social graces represent their power and their gift, but life demands balance and its just dues for the lack of it.

Procrastination and lack of self-discipline could lead to indulgence and problems affecting them in the kidneys.

2-7-9

Roger Oliver Lawrence Alma Beatrice Olive Jeaninne Sophie Rodney Anita Zahira Valerie Ahmad Jafar

Idealism and a desire to serve life are the prime motivating factors of these people. This is a soft and kindly influence. They would do anything to avoid conflict. This is not a hardy physical or hardworking quality. Only by using their social skills can they move ahead. They are the dreamers who wish that life was a place of love in a world devoid of suffering where everyone could live in peace and harmony.

There is so much idealism here that it is difficult for these types to fit into a world gone mad in a race to accomplish and to achieve merely for the sake of survival. The pressure of the marketplace does nothing to stimulate their naturally creative natures.

It is through the arts that they find an expression for their idealism. They could write, create music, or do anything as long as they are expressing their love for life and the people in it. Love is the thread that moves them to action in their endeavors. If there is not love, there is not life!

Even though they have a deep sentimental nature, they lack an inward depth. Because of this they can come across as being a little too flighty and a bit impractical. They have the gift of the gab and as much as they try, it is sometimes difficult to curb that urge. Consequently they can suffer from a reputation of being a little shallow.

If they possess deeper qualities in the rest of their make-up, they could become counselors because of their deep concern for others. Listening more and talking less could endear them to others because of a natural compassion for suffering humanity. This compassion on a universal scale moves them to serve and to give in some way to causes involved in world suffering. They are impressionable to panhandlers and others who see them as an easy mark. Any kind of suffering could cause them to give the very shirt off their backs. They are generous and accommodating.

In matters of personal love they can lose out if they do not understand the universality of their love—in that it must be expressed for the benefit of all, for a grander purpose than to satisfy a personal fancy.

It is not easy for these people to succeed in life unless it is through the artistic field. If they find life difficult, they soon lose confidence and become lazy and indulgent. Being so soft and easygoing, it is difficult to stand up for themselves. Procrastination is their downfall.

It is their overly idealistic nature that makes them dreamers who could give to life the benefit of their visions but who are usually looked upon as unrealistic. They crave love and affection and are romantics who look for a better life through books, music, movies, and the like.

It is through religious or philosophical thought that they could strive to understand and express their idealism.

Not being physically very robust, they must watch their diets and beware of over-eating and indulging in sweet foods. Their weakness lies in the kidneys and in the nervous system.

2-8-1

Noel Adam Joseph Rebecca Elaine Hannah Alan Arlene Sabrina Edmond Elliott Joey Lorne Zachary

While these people have many fine qualities, they are forced to cope with two opposite influences that work against each other. On the one hand, they draw from an urge to please and to serve others, while they are compelled by another force to exert their own strong views. They are both soft and accommodating as well as strong and independent. This sounds like a nice balance but it inadvertently creates difficulty in their lives.

Even as they express themselves verbally, they know that speech is not coming out or flowing as they feel it should. There is a candidness that belies their true intention. They mean one thing and say another. The truth is they have great difficulty in finding the right words at times. When this occurs they feel apologetic and usually say or dismiss their remarks with a laugh or humorous remark in order not to offend.

In their deepest desires they love to keep the peace between people. They are sensitive inwardly and are easily offended and hurt by unkind words. They are awkward in responding appropriately in difficult situations. Their blunt manner has an affect on others that they feel and regret. Their longing for a deep contact with others can be frustrated when there is difficulty understanding and communicating with others.

These conflicting forces have the effect of sometimes producing anti-social behavior because these people don't always feel they fit in. The opposing qualities tend to direct the mental focus primarily on their own life. It undermines the power of the intellect and the ease of debate. At times the approach will be to agree or submit in conversation, and at other times there is a display of stubbornness that will cause alienation.

On the positive side, these types can be loyal and steadfast in their associations. They have a great desire to help out wherever they can, and they will stick by what few friends they have under all circumstances.

This is a quality that is not deep or particularly philosophical and will therefore conform to the general trend of thought and the prevailing concepts of life.

They can be hard working, but because of this split in their character they must be careful to watch their health and their diet. They require periods of rest in between their work, otherwise their body will not withstand the rigors of too much physical exertion.

These people have a good heart and good intentions but may fail to demonstrate their affections to others.

Human consciousness is made up of different qualities or character traits, and success lies in knowing how to balance them. The balance of the name reveals our potential for accomplishment in all areas of life.

In health, these people have a weakness in the kidneys as well as in the senses of the head.

2-9-2

Catherine Sarah Marian Diana Violet Heather Adriene Adrian Dana Melody Norbert Dione Katrina Kamal

These people possess a quality of mind that makes them gracious, accommodating, and passive. This is a soft feminine influence that is warm and open and easily affected by any discord in the environment. They are like a sponge absorbing all that comes into their mental atmosphere. Their eagerness to please is not so much premeditated as it is an unconscious response to all people. They do it without thinking, as an impulse that could not be curbed even if they disliked a person. Their acquiescence is so complete that they tend to lose their own identity in their emotional response to all people. Their aim to please comes both from a genuine response as well as from a need to avoid conflict.

This is a quality of consciousness that is very attractive to the opposite sex because it is open and inviting, which makes it vulnerable to abuse. Their eyes reveal their openness and their charm. They have beautiful smiles. In the highest sense, they have the potential to make people feel relaxed and important because they easily listen to what others have to say. Drawing people out is so natural to them that without knowing why, individuals reveal their innermost thoughts to them. Their disarming personalities make everyone feel relaxed and welcome. They have an intuitive nature that is capable of discerning another's problems. If they could develop their minds they could become excellent counselors.

In these names there is so much of the accommodating quality that they are incapable of standing up for themselves. They have such a sensitivity to discord that they will do anything to avoid conflict. "Peace at all costs," could be their motto. They can be so agreeable that after a while they can sacrifice their own mental development through fear of expressing their own ideas. Eventually, if they are not observant, they will cease to have any ideas of their own. They must learn to cultivate an intellect, otherwise they can become shallow, lazy and inclined to gossip.

This is not a confident quality and is therefore forced to work for and with others. It is hard for them to get ahead in life because of the lack of initiative. Being submissive is a beautiful quality only when it is in balance.

The negative aspects of these names is in their lack of appreciation of time. They are invariably late and unaware and unconcerned of others' dependence on them in these matters. Their procrastination can become habitual when they become preoccupied with themselves and the little things that are inconsequential.

In the highest, this is the epitome of the feminine influence of softness and diplomacy.

For a man it tends to destroy the masculine force of positivity and self-confidence. They abhor getting their hands dirty.

This quality as a shade of consciousness governs the kidneys and fluid functions of the male and female. They will suffer from cold hands and feet because of poor circulation. Due to a lack of discipline over their appetites and little interest in exercise, they can become overweight.

3-1-4

Ruth Constance Wilbur Georgina Natalia Cordelia Rowena

As in so many cases, these names contain elements that are somewhat conflicting. Figuratively or literally they desire to be in the spotlight but always find themselves backstage doing all the work. In other words, they possess an inspiration that they cannot fully express outwardly.

They are not quite as demonstrative with their feelings as they would like to be. They can smile in response to a joke but cannot laugh deeply from the depths of their soul. In consequence, they fall short of reaching this usually unconscious response to their deeper nature. Even if they were to find themselves on the stage, they would find it difficult to deliver their lines with the depth of feeling that they would like.

In relationships it is difficult to express warmth and to be able to let go.

In spite of what has been said, this influence is a fairly balanced one. These people are responsible and hard working. They are always aware of the little things that need to be done in order to make life just a bit better. In fact this could be a source of aggravation for others. They have a sense of their own and other's imperfections when dealing with little details and tend to make much out of nothing. They must beware of being overly fussy about inconsequentials.

Their intellect is keen and they have a logical approach to life. Their minds look for the orderliness in things and their conversation is intelligent. It is through their minds that they can find success. They have the power to think, concentrate and work out solutions to problems. Their love of people draws them into many social involvements where others appreciate their practicality and willingness to take responsibilities.

This quality is not endowed with a great deal of confidence. Their success must be achieved through the academic route or in some specialized field where their studious ability and perseverance will see them through. If they do not utilize their studious potential for getting ahead then they will find themselves trapped in mundane pursuits. They can work hard but soon find that it becomes boring and too much like drudgery. It is their dual nature that draws them into social circumstances only to end up doing a lot of work—in retrospect they wonder how they got themselves into it. At times they feel an impulse to fly and be done with all the work, and the next moment they are trapped in the mundane again.

This other side of their nature just wants to be with people, experience their warmth and camaraderie, and not have to deal with work. They have quite a strong love nature that needs expression through art, music and dancing, otherwise it will express mostly on the physical level. They have the discipline to take lessons and to finish the things they start. Because of the dual aspect of their nature they will always feel the limitation of not being able to quite express the depth of their emotion. This repression will affect them somewhat throughout their lives.

Any tension in their lives will affect them through constipation and liver problems.

3-2-5

Rudy Russ Caroline Joanne
Samantha Cyrus Rosanne

These people have a great potential for creativity but seldom live up to it. They are clever, quick-minded, and spirited. They could become formidable in debate and intellectual pursuits but most often succumb to the negativity of their emotional natures. When this occurs, they do not listen to others but merely debate to hear themselves talk and fail to grasp the difference between debate and argument. Their quickness in response and thought makes one think that "they hear you but do not listen." Their eagerness to "self-express" makes them poor listeners. These people have a mind that is restless and ready to debate a point at the slightest provocation.

Their ire can be easily aroused and once into an argument it is impossible to bow out gracefully. They must have the last word.

This quality is emotional, very active, and unstable. Since it is their nature to be active, they can be quite temperamental and subject to moods of depression if they are repressed.

Their talents lie in any area where they can use their speech and their ability to motivate others. They are sales oriented and great promoters. Art and music inspire them, and they should pursue singing, dancing, or other art forms but seldom can they discipline themselves to follow through with their interests.

They are restless, ambitious, and quite independent. It is this emotional aspect that destroys their staying power. Their lives are a series of uncompleted projects. As soon as they see that they can do a job, they leave it for some new adventure. Further fields always look greener. Their versatility can move them into any number of fields and vocations. If there is sufficient balance in the rest of their make-up, they can accomplish great things. If not, then they merely acquire experiences and constant change, not realizing that change seldom constitutes progress.

They fail to understand that success is built upon a foundation of stability where the top is reached by building block upon block. Their motivation is inspiration; when patience and hard work is required they become bored and move on to new projects.

Their quickness of mind and keen perceptual skills could be used to their advantage; however, they often use them to criticize and challenge the things that irritate them.

They have courage and a daredevil side to their natures and are not afraid of taking a chance. These people are opportunists who can achieve great success and lose everything at the next turn. Their impulsiveness can sometimes work to their advantage, while at other times it becomes their nemesis. They can be fortunate but unstable.

Being emotional, they crave the affection of the opposite sex but find it difficult to stay in relationships. Their caustic tongue invariably leads to quarreling and differences that become irreconcilable.

Peace of mind eludes them as they are driven by forces that they cannot understand.

Their health suffers through digestive problems and liver afflictions. They must not consume alcohol.

3-3-6

Leonard Judy Dorothy Norton
Rosemary Veronica Dustin Cameron
Lorea Lorenda Leora
Mahara Rossanne

In so many instances, people are short-suited where they feel certain urges but are unfulfilled because they do not have the qualities needed to realize their ambitions. With the above names there are no such shortages. These names provide an artistic and expressive potential along with the confidence to succeed.

They have musical ability and a commitment to their art. Their strong sense of responsibility will see them through their efforts. Not only are they dedicated to their craft, but they are also natural mothers and fathers. Their paternal or maternal instincts make them excellent teachers and caregivers. If there is imbalance in the rest of their names, then their only problem is that their strong sense of knowing what is right or wrong can manifest as interference or bossiness.

Taking the initiative comes easy for these types. For this reason they can get ahead in life. They do not wait to be asked and are quickly promoted and recognized for their abilities. They love responsibility and naturally gravitate to the top of the ladder where they are strong enough to stand up to anyone who gets in their way. They are not pushy but quite helpful towards those who are less able. Nothing pleases them more than to teach others how to succeed. In their modesty they must be looked up to for their knowledge. Their nurturing capacities endear them to their fellowman.

One aspect of their character is a desire for music, singing, and dancing as a way of expressing an innate desire for fun, while the responsible aspect will never allow them to go overboard or take anything to extremes. They are serious and conscientious with a tendency to worry too much over inconsequentials. Crossing their bridges before they get to them could be a weakness if the rest of their names are unbalanced.

There is a great deal of intelligence in the above names. There is not much that they could not accomplish. Any deficiency in others is quickly detected by these people. Their mental perception is sharp and they would not hesitate to let others know where they are wrong in their concepts. They can usually do this without giving offense.

They could only be prevented from realizing their ambitions when there is imbalance in their entire make-up. If this is the case and they cannot reach positions of responsibility and leadership, they can be overbearing and interfering in other's efforts. If they have deserved the right as a true authority figure, they can do much to help others; if they have not, then their approach and attitude in conversation could get them the reputation of being know-it-alls.

There is nothing small-minded about these people. They are good in debate and seek out intelligent people as their friends. Their love of family and friends forms the basis for their lives.

They must consciously come to understand their natural sense of knowing the difference between right and wrong if they are to realize their potential as teachers and leaders.

This is a very healthy influence. If they carry too much responsibility they could suffer from anxiety and excessive worry.

3-4-7

Barbara Roberta Otto Burt Lucy Alanna Amanda Kurt Connor Penelope Luis Eloisa

When expressed to the highest, this quality is the epitome of gracefulness, rhythm, and harmony. Its deep sensitivity produces a great refinement through its appreciation for music, art and love of nature. At the deepest level, these people can be tuned to the most profound thoughts regarding the mystery of life because they are so finely tuned to its essence. This does not mean to say that they all naturally possess these qualities because if they are unbalanced, the negative side of over-sensitivity will manifest as an emotionalism that is very difficult to control.

This profound sensitivity unconsciously compels them to withdraw from the unpleasant situations of noise, confusion, and misunderstandings by turning inward and closing off or creating an impenetrable wall between themselves and others. This moodiness can cause them to become judgmental, and their unconscious manner of getting even is through an icy silence. They are easily offended and must seek deeply into their own psyche to understand the mystery and purpose of such a deep sensitivity. If they do not develop their mind and intellect, then they live almost exclusively in their feelings and their "sense" of mysticism. This can lead to a life of emotional indulgence—of seeking pleasure in order to assuage this unquenchable urge for love and understanding, or it can take them into flights of fantasy and mysticism, devoid of logic.

These people have a charm and a naturally romantic nature but can be put off at the drop of a hat over some crass remark because of this deep refinement and attunement to beauty and perfection. They are disarming by virtue of their openness and loving way. It is only later that one discovers their inability to make a conversation flow easily. They feel far more than they can communicate verbally. They are forced to look inward for the happiness that others can find and experience in easy association with others. Their unfathomable sensitivity defies understanding unless they can develop their minds along intellectual avenues. If they can do this, they can become profound thinkers. If not, they are led and become a prey to their own emotional natures. When this happens, at times they encounter thought forms and feelings that can be quite frightening.

This represents the challenge of sensitive types in that sensitivity can be either a blessing or a curse depending on the mind's ability to become the master controller.

Their natural outlet is through music and dancing.

Their sense of rhythm is so precisely tuned to music that they can flow with a gracefulness that is beautiful to observe. Their whole body moves with the soul of the music so that they become one with it. Nature, music, and movies can capture their imagination and hold them in a spell of inward joy that they cannot share with anyone for fear of being misunderstood.

They are idealists who must develop their minds. If unbalanced, they will be affected through moods of depression which will ultimately affect them through the heart, lungs and bronchial organs. They can also suffer through skin problems.

3-5-8

Hugh Guy Marjorie Loreta Georgia Burl Brooks Cassandra Deborah Marianna Samara Kurtis Curt Quincy

The balance in these names provides poise and self-confidence. These people are always cheery, with a good sense of humor. They are generally well liked and personable. Two aspects in their personalities balance quite nicely: their inherent appreciation of music combined with the urge to entertain and inspire others, and their business sense which allows them to manage or direct the affairs of others on some level.

This is an ambitious influence that needs to achieve a level of personal autonomy. They have big ideas and an appetite to match. Overindulgence could be their main problem.

If the rest of their names are balanced, there is nothing to stop these types. They will reach their goals because of their abilities and their positive approach to life. If they are going to be happy, they must become leaders in whatever they undertake.

Their understanding and feeling for people is exemplary. They have a way with others that is both kind and firm. Their love expresses through their contact with their associates. One cannot help but respond favorably to these types because of their warm personalities. Only if the rest of their names are unbalanced would their negative side express as a domineering or bossy quality, and this is only because they would not be able to succeed in life. They must achieve a certain financial independence before they are satisfied with their efforts.

They have a delightful stage presence, a confidence that comes across as if nothing could disturb them. In front of people, they are at their best whether telling a joke or entertaining by singing or speaking. They are not too emotional, so their presentation comes across in a very poised manner. Their commanding presence draws attention and their warmth creates a sympathetic connection.

They are masters at using humor to disarm a potentially difficult situation. Seeing the funny side of things comes naturally to them. If they have not developed their musical or artistic side, it would then express through emotional excesses, usually through food.

Their intelligence and mental objectivity make them good leaders. They do not easily become ruffled. It is beneath them to be drawn into argument. Being able to maintain this dispassionate connection with emotional types, allows them to see clearly what is taking place. Their eternal optimism sees them through their difficult moments.

Whatever business they engage in, they must be

the boss, otherwise they will never be totally happy. Normally this is a very balanced quality. If there is a fault, it is in a preoccupation with the material plane. They have rich tastes and sometimes develop a wealth complex that leads them to surround themselves with the best things money can buy. They are dignified and their speech is cultured and clear.

While this could be a good quality for both male and female, it can at times be a little too masculine for a woman. She could find her relationships with men quite competitive.

This is quite a healthy influence. If their indulgence in rich foods is not controlled, they will suffer from liver or generative disorders.

3-6-9

Judith Curtis Bud Carole Tamara Mohammed Francoise Luc Angelo Mahalia Alastair

These people are motivated by their idealism and their desire to do something useful in life for the benefit of others. Through service in life we have hope of experiencing the highest goal attainable by any human—love.

Passion and compassion are the two strongest motivating forces in the lives of those with the above names. This is a very emotional quality; sometimes they are influenced by passion and at other times they feel the suffering of others and are drawn by compassion to help the needy. The challenge they continually confront is the commanding desire for love and affection. Their passions are strong and to borrow a Christian term, "their flesh is weak."

Personal love can become a preoccupation. They can be absolutely consumed with the experience of "falling in love." When this happens their inspiration moves them to great heights of generosity and kindness. Of course this is impossible to maintain.

Their compassion can be awakened through human suffering, and in this way they can learn to understand how to enter into a passionate embrace with life and love in a broader and more universal sense. They will then also begin to understand the more complex issue involving intimacy with the opposite sex and the nurturing element that is experienced when the goal in a couple's life is beyond themselves.

Being emotional and quite sentimental, these types swing in their moods from inspirational highs to lows that bring depression and self-pity. Through losses in their affections, it takes them forever to move past their grief. They are prone to jealousy and fits of temper.

They are always responsive to kindness and will reciprocate in kind. They are romantics and dreamers and deeply moved by a good book or movie where there is love, tragedy, or when their heart strings are touched in any way. They must sing and dance in order to bring out their love natures along creative channels.

Their sympathy with others' problems make them good listeners and counselors. At heart they are teachers provided they can learn that it is wisdom that must be given and not merely a sympathetic ear. If they become overly sympathetic, then people will use them to dump all their miseries and problems. They are usually compelled to give much more than they ever receive. Their greatest lesson is to give wisdom.

They have the power to inspire others with their

love but only if they develop their talents and their wisdom. In their ability to inspire an audience, the spoken word lies as their greatest potential.

Their emotions represent their greatest struggle. If the rest of their make-up tends to accentuate this emotional condition, they never develop or succeed but fall prey to emotional indulgence. They feel everything so deeply that disappointments can cause them to easily give up on their ambitions. Although they are motivated by inspiration, they do not have a great deal of confidence or self-discipline and do not usually have the staying power to follow through with their projects. If they become too emotional their liver and their nervous system will suffer.

3-7-1

Gordon Buck Loretta Woody Natasha Roxanne Ambrose Guri Tatyana Coretta Chuck

Self-confidence, expressiveness and determination are some of the more positive characteristics of these names. The keynote would be self-expression. While this is quite a good numerical influence generally, we jokingly accuse them of suffering from "hoof-and-mouth disease." Their fluid verbal expression combined with their need to have the last word can sometimes catch them with their foot in their mouth. They have a quickness of mind that finds expression through their tongue. Combine these two elements and you have a formidable debater. Throw in their natural sense of humor and you find that they love to tease but sometimes they do not know when enough is enough.

Their combined qualities of self-expression and strong self-assertiveness may overshadow their ability to listen and this may create problems in relationships. This gift of verbal spontaneity can either be an asset or a liability depending on the overall balance of their names. If there is sufficient balance, these people can become quite successful because they have plenty of initiative and drive. They have a love of people as well as a strong independent streak that finds them doing things their own way.

They could do well at anything that utilizes their speech; in fact, it is through their speech that they get ahead in life—that is, if they have learned to curb this outspoken manner that can sometimes offend others.

Theirs is a carefree attitude that hates to be tied down to detail and routine. They love change and travel with a little bit of excitement thrown in. When they are free and independent, they are at their best creatively and can do anything within their natural interests. If they are tied down or confined in any way, then the negative aspects of stubbornness and their argumentative natures will come out.

As children they are not easy to discipline. It is this strong sense of individuality that seeks its own way through life. Their creativity will always find a channel through originality. They desire to be free and work to become their own bosses, independent and self-sufficient.

At times they may seem arrogant, but their self-confidence and clever minds are often ahead of others. They are not afraid to stand firm in their ideas, however, they must learn to give credit to others' thoughts, otherwise they will show a level of intolerance that will not stand them in good stead.

These names are quite balanced by themselves;

however, if the surname produces imbalance then the ensuing frustration can make these people critical, sarcastic, and difficult to live with because nothing seems to satisfy them. At these times they can become incessant complainers.

If there is an overall balance, they are usually quite healthy with only a susceptibility to liver ailments and a tension that will affect them through the senses of the head.

3-8-2

Gus Lorraine Leona Lenora Elanor

These names love to inspire others through music, singing and dancing. These soft, easygoing, and diplomatic people also possess an affectionate disposition that makes them gregarious, sensitive, and understanding of others' feelings. Their whole motivation in life is based upon their need for loving relationships.

Unfortunately they lack both the practicality and the discipline to carry out their ambitions to a successful conclusion. If there is imbalance or weakness in the rest of their make-up, they will find life quite difficult. While they should be singing and dancing, their lack of ambition usually sees them frittering their time away in rather shallow pursuits. Their oversensitivity destroys the confidence needed to initiate creative projects. They will wait for opportunities to come to them without realizing the tremendous effort required to succeed at anything. Their ship may never come in because of an exaggerated idealism and a dream that cannot be realized for want of positivity and strength of mind through balance.

These types are very social, warm and affectionate, with charm and a smile that is loving and very captivating. They need to understand the power of this charismatic quality in order to influence others in a positive and constructive way. Their lesson is to learn about love in the highest, or they will suffer the consequences of indulging in love as a purely emotional feeling. Their need to be loved and embraced can become an obsession.

This is not an intellectual force in any way, and therefore, lives in and for emotional sensation. They need the discipline to pursue an artistic career or they tend to become lazy and procrastinating. The lack of drive must be overcome if they are to find themselves through art. Only through many years of effort does the very spirit of anything make itself known. Follow-through is not a strong point within these names.

Blending into a conversation or into the atmosphere of others is natural and easy for them. This is a passive force that understands the feelings of others and listens with interest and understanding. They could become counselors because of this intuitive element that allows them to understand the nature of others' problems. Their advice is often just what is needed. Unfortunately, they have a hard time following or living-up to this advice in their own lives.

Making others feel relaxed comes naturally. One easily falls in love with these people because of such an open quality. It invites others to come in. Sadly, they are taken advantage of because of their soft accommodating personalities. Their strong need for love makes them impressionable and dependent on others.

House work and manual labor, like mathematics and anything that requires attention to detail, is abhorrent to them.

Indulgence in sweet foods can lead to a breakdown in their health through kidney and liver problems.

3-9-3

Ruby Quinn Rosaline Charlotte Sunny Alexander Justin Adriana Tatiana Francesco

The lives of these people are moved by emotion and inspiration. Their minds weave an image of life based upon imagination, idealism, and love. They are sensitive, talkative, and usually full of fun. Practicality is something that is almost entirely absent from their lives. If they are ever going to succeed it is through the use of their imagination.

Music, writing, and the arts are the only channels that could constructively satisfy their emotional natures. Unfortunately, discipline is extremely difficult for them to acquire, and their lives may end up as an exercise in futility.

They are motivated by inspiration to follow a multitude of different interests, and when the work begins, boredom quickly sets in. Finishing the things they start is their biggest obstacle. When inspiration needs to be replaced by routine and hard work, they become deflated and their mind looks toward new adventures. Taking lessons in anything is usually short lived.

Whether as a child or adult, they must play. They

are shy, sensitive, and easily hurt, but in an environment of friends, they can be full of humor and mischief. Any opportunity to play games brings out their loving nature. People who are good at telling jokes love these types because they will laugh at anything and their laughter is infectious.

Affection is the mainspring of their existence. They love all people and all things, but their shyness often causes them to withdraw onto safer ground. Sometimes when attention is focused on them, their faces can become flushed with embarrassment, and blushing can be a problem throughout their lives. At other times, they can be the life of the party. The feelings of love well up within them when they can sing and dance. If they could overcome their sensitivity and develop discipline, they could inspire people to great heights through music and art.

If they cannot discipline themselves, then their scattered and emotional natures turn to indulgence. They can become great complainers about every little thing that bothers them. Their intolerance can eventually drive others away from them. Having the gift of the gab, their need for self-expression can make them poor listeners. They are easily drawn into argument.

Being so emotional, their thinking is usually colored by their strong feelings in any given circumstance. Their minds are not strong or intellectual. They lack concentration and can't remember where they have left things to save their soul. They are happy-go-lucky and things usually turn out for them because of it.

Doing any kind of work that requires physical labor or attention to details is abhorrent to them. Only if work can be made into a game can they pursue it.

It is their purpose to use their power of love and inspiration to influence others. If they do not, then this power will manifest as an insatiable urge for affection, sex, and indulgence in food.

Even though at times their emotions will drag them down into depression, they have a basic optimism that brings them up quickly. Because of this, it could be said that they are fortunate but unstable. They are prone to liver and skin diseases.

4-1-5

Paul Arthur Prudence Claud Suria Lemuel

These people are practical, materialistic, and exacting in every detail of their lives. They are logical in their approach to all things and skeptical of theories that have not been tried and proven. Religion is often viewed with derision and even contempt, unless it makes sense and appeals to the intellect. Here we have an interesting duality of qualities. On the one hand, there is a desire for a patient, unhurried, and stable life style, while they are continually driven by another aspect of their nature which is very difficult to reconcile with the former.

No detail escapes these people in their personal pursuits. They have a great capacity for hard work. Their life may be seen as an enquiry into the many aspects of their restless natures—a restlessness that can drive them to distraction. It usually finds an outlet in the more practical avenues of life, or if they develop philosophically, they can travel the world looking for answers. Unfortunately, they are never satisfied for long before they are off again seeking something new to fulfill this insatiable urge for peace of mind and stability. These conflicting forces invariably affect them in the stomach and intestinal tract.

Their focus and concentration, combined with their perseverance, makes them dedicated workers. In fact, these are the types who could become workaholics.

They are serious types who lack a sense of humor, with little appreciation for the more aesthetic and inspirational side of life. Their skepticism for anything that is unproven, alienates them from the idealistic types of people. They immerse themselves in their work rather than spend time in social activities. Their penchant for detail and facts along with their natural skepticism can make them dull conversationalists.

Their creativity comes from an intense and concentrated effort. Nothing can deter these people when their minds are set on a particular course. They can pursue the minutest detail to discover an answer to a problem. They will drive themselves for so long and then new horizons beckon. After a while they discover that all they have ever wanted is to settle down and create stability, yet this they will find almost impossible.

This practical, deliberate, and slow moving quality comes in conflict with an underlying influence of change and becomes a challenge that produces so much dis-ease and frustration in their lives.

They must work hard to bring softness and inspiration into their character, otherwise their relationships will suffer. Neglect of an overall balance can make these people overly materialistic and blind to their own weaknesses because of a hardness that can creep into their natures.

There is no denying their natural abilities in research and hard work, but it is at the cost of their physical and mental well-being.

Their level of imbalance can eventually affect their stomach and intestines producing constipation, ulcers and other allied problems.

4-2-6

Murray Truman Demetrius
Lucian Raymund

Persistence, patience, and a steadfast determination form the basis for these people's character. They have a concern for others and a strong sense of responsibility to their friends and to their tasks.

Their focus is mostly on the material plane; they are not usually deep or philosophical. If anything, their deeper convictions about life will follow traditional values. Their endurance and penchant for work demonstrates their reliability and loyalty. They are physically strong, and because of their positive attitude towards work, they naturally conserve their energy.

This is not an emotional influence. If they are emotional because of other aspects of their names or their birth date, it will go strongly against the grain. Nothing is more desirable than having and living a life free from any kind of turmoil.

These types crave the stability and regularity of a well-ordered life. They have the ability to work out all the necessary details of their day. Planning and routine are essential to their daily life. If this routine is disturbed, they can become quite upset. When this happens they display a streak of stubbornness and a resistance to change.

They are not easily adaptable to pressure or to change. Their motto could be, "slow and steady wins the race." They don't mind working long and hard, but they cannot be pushed.

Their patience can see them through many difficult times. Somehow they know that their perseverance will win out in the end, or perhaps they realize that there is nothing else to do but keep on working.

With these people there is no great idealism or lofty visions. They are skeptical of new ideas or philosophical theories. Only with the stamp of academia do new ideas become credible in their minds and worthy of notice or attention.

They are not versatile or deep thinking, but they could pursue research because of their basic or logical approach to things. Facts alone appeal to and awaken a response in their minds. Their intellectual ability is directed mostly to those things which come into the realm of the five senses.

They do not have great conversational ability. Their talk is usually concerned around their work or other practical matters. Their imbalance lies in their preoccupation with materiality, although they do have a strong sense of responsibility to home and family.

Their concern for what is right for people and their own family can involve them in community affairs. They are not selfish, but need to cultivate inner wisdom. Their responsible natures compel them to do the proper thing.

It is most desirable for them to be their own boss because they do not respond well to working in a subordinate role. They do have the potential for success, provided the rest of the name has some balance.

In relationships they are not very flexible. Because of their potential lack of depth, marital difficulties are seldom resolved satisfactorily. Work or hobbies are usually their means of escape from having to deal with the deeper questions concerning personal intimacies.

Worry can be a problem with them, as well as constipation and its ensuing problems.

4-3-7

Antonio Jonathon Osvaldo Avolon

The vast majority of people who view the extremes in human character have no idea why this is so. The truth is, our minds are created through language, and our shortcomings are deeply rooted in our names. Like musical notes, some names create discord when combined, while others produce a chord of harmony. The above names are quite unbalanced.

There are two influences in these names that do not balance. The main quality of practicality, science, and materiality is drawn toward the physical plane exclusively. The remaining influence is theoretical, quiet and contemplative. Unfortunately, since they do not support each other, they tend to bring out the worst in each other.

The depth of the one influence is destroyed and the intellectual force of the other produces an instinctual response to life. It results in a heavy materialistic tendency with little interest in the deeper aspects of life. There is a preoccupation with getting and spending, and a general focus on the mundane duties of everyday life. They lean towards mechanical, electrical and other practical fields of work.

This is not a vibrant or social influence. No matter how hard they try to create friends and meaningful conversation, it does not happen often. They are looked upon as quite boring to be with. Their minds work on a very pragmatic level and their speech is monotone. They are slow and methodical in their conversation and must stop to think about everything before they speak. While others are on to a new topic, they are still pondering the last thought. Skepticism and a general lack of interest in other's thoughts becomes a way of life.

They are destined to experience loneliness; they lack the spontaneity and social rapport of others and consequently withdraw into their own world. Potentially they possess a studious quality and would do well to cultivate their interests through mathematics, astronomy, and scientific research, or spend their lives fiddling with hobbies to no avail. Being earthy types, gardening could also be a constructive outlet for them.

It is unfortunate that their love relationships, if they had any, become predominantly physical experiences. Giving to others as a love response is not a strong part of their character. They have such a strong self-orientation that love relationships would be difficult to build or sustain. Conversations would be quickly reduced to talking about domestic duties. There is no incentive for intellectual stimulation and their life would soon revert back to their own limited interests.

There is little self-confidence here, and little desire for conversation. In time, their introversion can create an antisocial attitude, not so much from lack of desire, but from failure to achieve and experience positive results for their efforts.

Hopefully, the rest of their make-up will modify some of the negative characteristics that have been outlined. Constipation and problems affecting their heart, lungs and bronchial organs are their physical weaknesses.

4-4-8

Saul Angus Julia Gertrude Callum Judah Guiseppe

B ehind these names lies a quality that produces a very practical nature. These people live according to a pattern or systematic routine. Everything in their lives is orderly and planned. Nothing can be out of place.

Their values are based upon material pursuits and hard work which they are quite capable of. They don't miss a detail in their effort to complete their chores. Everything has to be precise, neat, and tidy.

They make good bookkeepers, housekeepers, or accountants and can do anything that requires research and attention to detail. They are reliable, fastidious and patient workers. Slow and methodical would be their key quality. To them success is just a matter of hard work, patience, and waiting, with the emphasis on waiting. Because they know they can finish the things they start, they can live by the adage that "All things come to those that wait."

This quality is neither inspirational nor endowed with a great deal of confidence. It is their hard work alone which sees them make slow and systematic progress.

If these people have a naturally inspirational path through their time of birth, then they will be quite repressed because these names compel them into the practical fields. If such were the case, the worst of their dual nature would express through being over-emotional as well as being extremely fussy. When other elements within their combined names do allow for some artistic expression, it will come out in a rather mechanical way.

These names show a rather predominant influence of practicality with an absence of idealism making them somewhat materialistic and concerned mainly with the mundane aspects of daily living. They could become fussy and preoccupied with the incidentals of life to the exclusion of the more aesthetic values.

Their bent is toward science, home, hobbies, and information that is practical. They are skeptical about anything in life that does not have the stamp of approval from academia.

Being sticklers for detail, they could be quite demanding and nit-picking without much capacity for bending. There is very little versatility here or desire for new experiences. They are shrewd, calculating, and tight with their money.

Getting ahead in life with these types is usually measured in terms of the size of their bank account. They would only consider doing something else once they had achieved financial independence.

Because of the one-sided aspect of these names, it is difficult for them to be happy and content. Lacking humor and spontaneity, they tend to be quiet and would rather spend time alone than have to respond to people. Their discussion would pertain to such things as plumbing, gardening, politics, or the best way to save a dollar.

Their greatest desire would be to have their own business where they could do things their own way and not have to put up with people who do not have their penchant for detail and order.

The predominance of this practical element can lead to problems affecting them through constipation and allied problems as well as in the generative area.

4-5-9

Stuart Julias Dorothia Shaun Theodore Darius Marius Anu Annamaria

This influence tends to make these people rather physical, and at the same time they can respond to the impulse within themselves through acts of giving and generosity.

The physical element robs them of the sensitivity required to understand people. They can be pushy without much regard for the feelings of others. Only in retrospect can they perceive the error of their ways, and then some of them still cannot see anything wrong in their conduct.

They can be heavy of body, however this does not necessarily mean heavy in the sense of weight. There is a materialism that governs and influences their direction in life. They are practical and fascinated with science and all things that represent form and mathematics. They have an intellectual approach to life that is oriented toward fact and logic and are quite skeptical of anything that is out of the realm of orthodoxy.

Hard work is not foreign to their natures; their plodding patience will persevere to the end. A preoccupation with work will cloud their vision of a greater purpose in life because their work is all for the sake of self. Unless they direct their lives toward scientific enquiry, it is likely that their lives will become rather humdrum in their treadmill existence of getting and spending purely for the sake of survival. Even though they lack the passion and the inspiration of the idealists of life, there is no doubt about their reliability and their endurance in the tasks they undertake.

There is a social side to their character in that they require the company of people. This is not a deep or philosophical quality. Their conversations will deal with the common subjects of the day or anything that is practical and has a leaning toward their material pursuits.

The emotional aspect to their character can express through music or art as long as there is balance in the other facets of their total make-up. Usually what occurs is an indulgence in their emotions because their physical aspect predominates. At times they can be quite giving and moved to do something humanitarian and experience glimpses of inspiration.

Their love of nature is also affected by their strong physical orientation and tends to express itself primarily on the physical plane. They may be moved by the love response between the male/female attraction, but it is very difficult to move it upward and develop a relationship of respect and mental stimulation. In close association the atmosphere they create becomes rather dull and a bit heavy, soon losing any inspiration that might have been there initially. In this case the conversation drops to talking about domestic requirements and becomes impossible to lift. Only when the mind is stimulated by a higher pursuit can there ever be love.

If their mind becomes bogged down in mediocrity, these types tend to indulge in their physical appetites. When this occurs their bodies are affected through stomach and intestinal problems.

4-6-1

Alfonso Judas Cassius Eunise Badru Juan Lukas Klaus Lucinda

The influence here is entirely materialistic and physical. If the true nature of any of these people is inspirational according to the birth date, they will be frustrated indeed. They are hard working and if there is any success, it is purely by the sweat of their brows. Things do not come easily for them.

There is not much that is inspirational here; it is all practicality. Their interests lie in mechanics, business, computers, mathematics, accounting, or anything that deals with fact and form.

This is a humorless quality that tends to lean heavily on the physical side of life. Even their bodies tend to become heavy with time and a meat-and-potatoes diet. They are not interested in religious pursuits unless they follow traditional values. Their minds cannot easily follow philosophical theory. They are not sensitive to the mystery of life, only to their most basic material and physical needs. They are survivalists and skeptical of anything that does not come within the range of the five senses.

They have an attunement with motors and machines that allows them to know when something is wrong. Patience and persistence are integral to their character. Their plodding natures remind us of the story of the tortoise and the hare—patience always wins out in the end.

These types must be left alone to struggle in their own way and in their own time. They will not be pushed and they are not adaptable. Their independence can be inscrutable. Compromise is not generally in their thinking. They are slow, methodical and determined to push on regardless of the obstacles—a bit like plough horses.

In social environments, if the discussion is not concerning business or material things, they lose interest or become skeptical. Working away by themselves is just fine. They are not bold or adventuresome. This is an earthy quality that likes to putter around the house or workplace fixing anything that needs repair.

No great vision or ambition motivates these people beyond the desire to get ahead personally and materially. They do have a pioneering nature that lends itself to originality of thought whether it is in the yard or in the laboratory. Through their concentration and meticulous enquiry, they can be quite inventive as long as they are left alone to do things in their own way.

They are not romantics. There is a certain insensitivity to the needs of the more aesthetic types. The male/female attraction is mostly satisfied physically.

The concept of balance through language and

name has to be the greatest mystery known to mankind. These name combinations contain a predominance of only one aspect of the spectrum of human consciousness, and consequently, these people will suffer from the lack of balance or wholeness.

Head tension and constipation are the main problems afflicting these people's physical bodies.

4-7-2

Susan Murial Hubbard Lucas Janus Malu

The main characteristics here are friendliness and cooperation. Unfortunately, they lack the two ingredients that lead to true personal success: confidence and drive. It is on the strength of their academic credentials, not on any personal initiative, that they can make some progress. Their easygoing natures balk at being pushed and they cannot handle pressure.

They are personable and diplomatic and make the perfect host or hostess by making guests feel relaxed and at home. How others feel in their company is very important to them. Drawing people out and listening is their natural way.

The influences here are not deep or intellectual unless they are related to academia. They do have the ability to study and concentrate to some degree but are not interested in plumbing the depths of life's mysteries. Their conversation usually revolves around people and things rather than ideas and theories. They must guard against being pulled into gossip and talking about little nothings forever and a day.

They have a fluidity of speech that reveals itself in

discussions dealing with the simple pleasantries of the day. This again is due to an early realization that it is better to stay away from discussions which might prove controversial or embarrassing. In the end their associations could become shallow and pointless.

Balance is the issue here. Their accommodating and sensitive natures tend to become a liability. Their fear of creating trouble and the consequent hurt feelings ultimately produce an attitude of avoidance. Attempting to please others is a wonderful quality only if it is not an escape from going deeper into a discussion and a relationship. These people are so easily affected by elements in the atmosphere of others that they might habitually do anything to keep things light and airy.

Generally these types do not succeed but end up in dead-end jobs pushing paper around forever. They are reliable and capable of working for others in this capacity. Working with detail is easy for them. It is their soft, easygoing natures and their fear of responsibility that soon destroys any ambition that may have been there initially.

Their self-depreciation undermines their confidence and gradually they can become lazy-minded. Procrastination tends to be their main fault; it is difficult to be on time when life has become too humdrum.

Their potential lies in their ability to counsel others. They possess an intuitive ability when listening to others. It is their challenge to develop their intellect in order to provide others with necessary information and not merely to console them in their misery.

Self-discipline is not their strong point. Being overweight can be a problem. These names do not lend themselves to health and well-being. They are prone to constipation and problems affecting the kidneys and fluid functions. If they do not get enough exercise, they will suffer from poor circulation with the resulting cold hands and feet.

4-8-3

Duncan Austin Marcus Eunice Dunstan Maud Tatum

These names represent an interesting mixture of forces. Even though they are fairly balanced, some difficulty may be experienced through two conflicting elements. There is a desire to be organized and have everything in order, but as hard as they try, things still end up in disarray.

While their outward expression and response to others is quite jovial, they will always be aware that something is missing. They cannot quite respond from the depths of their soul. In the expression of music or dance, they feel the confines of their creativity as they attempt to get a favorable response from their audience. Some people laugh from their very belly or solar plexus; these people laugh from the head, so to speak, rather than from their heart. They fall short of making a connection that feels so good and complete when the outward expression comes forth from the soul.

At times, they can focus remarkably well on details; while at other times, they desire to let go and be free from responsibilities and the cares of the day. Even though this duality may seem desirable, it has the effect of creating mixed desires. These two natures combine the need for artistic expression along with the need for inquiry into the practical and even the more scientific aspects of life. It is not impossible to reconcile the two, but it is not easy. If they enter into the field of music, they will focus on doing things exactly as they should be done according to the book.

Lacking in confidence, they must pursue their goals with meticulous accuracy. Everything must be followed step by step. Their confidence can only be gained by following things according to the logic or patterns that are laid out—they cannot "wing it." There is a certain lack of spontaneity that destroys some level of the natural artist in them.

They are friendly and helpful with a certain sense of good humor and camaraderie. Their love of people expresses in their willingness to help out wherever they can. They are not afraid of work when it involves people and a chance to socialize. Their conversation is easy.

Their interests are not particularly deep or philosophical but neither are they small-minded. Logic is the basis for their discussions. The practical element of their minds seeks out the logic in everything. Nothing passes their attention that is not logical. Their debating ability is keen because their astute minds work on the basis of fact, and they have no trouble expressing themselves verbally.

The one problem here is that their level of skepticism and their lack of depth could limit their involvement in life. They will either dismiss the more theoretical aspects of life in their conversations with others or refute anything that does not come within the range of their interests. At this point they must guard against becoming argumentative and stubborn.

Tension in their lives will affect them in the intestinal tract and the skin.

4-9-4

Julian Dugald Donovan Abdul Anastasia Octavio

These people cover an aspect of human consciousness that deals with form and fact. With them life should be a neat and tidy package. This is a quality that sees life through mathematics and order. No matter what they undertake in life, every part of the operation or piece in the puzzle must have its place.

They exemplify the greatest virtue of all: patience. To the more inspirational types, working with detail can become a distraction, while these people can actually find pleasure in it.

Even though all life and progress are based upon practical principles, there is the more theoretical and philosophical side of life that these people find difficult to grasp. They function from the basis of scientific enquiry; they lack, should we say, the mystical sensitivity that opens the mind to a fascination with religious and philosophical speculations. These people are limited in their interests to those things that deal exclusively with the five senses. If other aspects of their make-up draw them into religion, they still must have some sort of tangible proof of its logic before they will follow it.

Research, computers, mathematics, or anything requiring attention to detail interests these types. They see everything that is out of place in life. They are masters of precision, slow and methodical in their undertakings. Hard work does not deter them from accomplishing their goals. Unfortunately their lives are all hard work.

This influence is quite one sided and skeptical of things that do not have the stamp of approval from academia. They could be fussy to the extreme. If their true nature through their birth date happens to be inspirational, then they will also suffer to the extreme. These names lack in themselves the ability to respond with humor and spontaneity in general discussions. They tend to look for the logic of a joke. It is very difficult for them to experience any outward display of emotion. The unconscious suppression of the other sides of their nature can lead them to feel quite discontent at times.

Their intellectual minds require discussions that pertain to science, mechanics, or anything to do with the material world. They are not particularly ambitious. Anything that needs to be fixed, they can fix. The material world can become a preoccupation and all the little things that do not account for very much can become all-consuming. Their workshop and their hobbies can become an escape from having to deal with the whole of life.

Reliability and endurance make these people good employees. Their concentration and patience are invaluable in sorting out the details of any problem dealing with the practical side of life.

The imbalance of these names brings a heaviness to their character that makes their lives quite difficult. Typically "... they cannot see the forest for the trees." Their lack of a greater vision in life is overwhelmed by their material pursuits.

The stomach and intestinal tract are affected in their imbalance. Constipation can become a serious problem.

5-1-6

Herb Fred Denis Clive Shirley Peggy Millie Suzanna Claudia Paula Vincent Kristen Riley

As a rule these people are superachievers. They are responsible and capable of accomplishments beyond most others. Versatility, confidence, and drive are the main characteristics of these types. Unfortunately, they are often driven and cannot slow down. In this distracted state, they are prone to self-destruction in one form or another. If they can remain on the straight and narrow, their achievements number many times more than the rest of us. They hunger for new experiences and are motivated by the search for truth. Even so, peace of mind eludes them.

Only when they are motivated by the ideal of justice and truth and have a noble cause to live for can they experience a lasting sense of fulfillment. They are consciously or unconsciously drawn to circumstances where they see injustice and are forced, or compelled, to fight for what is right. More than once in their lives their stand on principle ends in their demise.

They can sense an untruth from the level of their

solar plexus and respond on an impulse almost beyond their control. A total disregard for any consequence makes them the true fighters after justice. It is for them to right the wrongs of humanity. In the fight they must distinguish between the anger and the truth or become lost in getting even, and therefore lose sight of reason.

They are extremely independent and self-sufficient and function on the basis of personal freedom. If there is no challenge in their work, change is imminent. In fact, if there is little stability in the rest of their make-up, their lives can be a series of uncompleted tasks. Their interest remains only as long as there is a challenge; when the challenge has been met, further fields begin to look greener. In some cases where there is too much imbalance and there is not the confidence to move on, then the level of frustration can lead to mental problems or a breakdown of the mind.

This is a very intellectual force with an astute perception and a quick mind. They can rise up the ranks quickly because they will take the initiative and not wait to be asked. If they cannot get their way, they will start their own venture.

Their cleverness has a weakness: they do not totally digest their thoughts. They think they know the truth of something because their minds perceive a thought intellectually, but their restlessness does not allow them to take the thought to a deeper level. Because of this, they miss the point behind their accomplishments and happiness is still an elusive commodity in their lives.

They long for stability and an answer to the mystery and meaning of life. Travelling and new adventures are a momentary distraction to their deep restlessness. When they get excited about a new project their minds become so active that sleep can be impossible. The same happens when they are affected by personal problems. Their minds become distracted through worry, and they are prone to insomnia.

When balanced these people possess a versatility that can take them into music and the arts or into business and the sciences. They are promoters and super salespeople.

5-2-7

Glenn Nell Henry Lynne Laurence Winifred Terri Kevan Lindsey Giles Bevin Jacqueline

These people are characteristically quiet, reclusive and independent. While hiking, exploring, and communing with nature they can find themselves for a moment. They feel an aversion to crowds and the shallowness of empty conversation. They need the company of the more intellectual types. Their minds are continually playing with thoughts of getting away from it all and moving to places of tranquillity and peace.

Even if they are able to create a haven for themselves away from the confusion of the crowd, they soon discover that all is not well. In the depths of their being there lies an element that drives them to wonder about life and its meaning. If they do not have an outlet for this restless feeling, they can be very hard on themselves and others. They can be moody and uncommunicative and at times caustic and blunt in their manner.

They are deep and reflective and need a peaceful environment if they are to be the creative people that their potential indicates. They can be either highly creative in their thoughts or extremely pessimistic depending upon their overall balance.

They are philosophical and suspicious of religious rhetoric, dogma, or ceremony. There is no pretense in their natures, and they can see through the sham in an instant. Tolerance of others' views is not their strong point. They are quick to take others up on their foolishness, or they can dismiss them in an instant.

Like a Henry Ford or a Henry Thoreau, they have an ingenuity without bounds, but if the rest of their make-up is too unbalanced they will not be happy. In fact, happiness is the elusive commodity in their lives.

They must create through writing and philosophical thought, if they are to find any semblance of peace. It is through writing that they can open up to something profound and creative, otherwise they wander the earth, literally or figuratively, seeking happiness, which is like trying to catch the elusive butterfly.

They could never work with or for others very successfully unless they are left alone to do things in their own way. Relationships are not easy for them for they do not easily tolerate fools. They often sense more than they could ever put into words. Too much talking can be very exhausting for them.

Their minds are quick and sharp; they have a versatility that could be directed into almost any field, but they must have their independence. Nature and the out-of-doors is their freedom and a source for recharging their body energies.

When repressed these people become antisocial. Their introversion that could lead them into a life of skepticism and a disinterest in people generally. Their health is then affected through the heart, lungs and bronchial area.

If these people are social by virtue of their inner nature through their birth date, then they will be repressed indeed.

5-3-8

Wendy Eric Keith Laura Cheryl Beth Jess Beryl Heidi Susanna Vince Tyler Bryce Eli Yves Betsy

These people are highly motivated achievers; they are ambitious and career oriented. Their goal is to become financially independent. Good business sense and an ability to manage money is their natural forte. They are self-motivated, hard working, and driven. They can accomplish a great deal but find it almost impossible to slow down.

These people have keen minds for investment and an astute business sense. If they are mothers and housewives, one can be sure they handle the money and handle it well. There is a shrewdness here and an ability to handle people. Organizing others comes easy as they are confident and positive with a good understanding of people.

They need to be in positions of leadership and management or running their own business. "Think big and think success" is their motto. If the rest of their name inhibits this quality and they find themselves working in a subordinate role, there could be no end to their frustration. Then they would become difficult to work with and also very hard on themselves because this is a very strong force.

They love a challenge and thrive in an atmosphere of competition. Sports can serve as an important and necessary outlet for their nervous energy. The only way they can slow down when they drive themselves is through some strenuous physical exertion. When these people get worked up, it is impossible to sleep. They cannot stop their minds; they are restless and dynamic but a peaceful mind is not within the realm of their experience. They are inventive and persistent and make excellent promoters and salespeople with their ability to motivate others.

For women, this quality can make them quite aggressive and self-contained to the point that marriage relationships become difficult. They do not fit into the traditional female role. They can look after themselves without the help or interference of a man. Their strength can be intimidating to most men. This quality can make them a little bit hard.

Even for the man, he should be careful that he does not become domineering and materialistic and lose the soft touch that is so important in relationships. If the elements of softness are in the other parts of his make-up, they could modify the hardness of this first name influence.

They do not lack for much in the world of materiality, but they have to learn to use their power and their wealth wisely.

On the higher side, this quality embraces justice

and fair play; on the lower side it can become unscrupulous and self-serving in the rise to power.

Nothing but the best satisfies their taste in clothing, food, and the luxuries of life. If there is too much imbalance here, they are prone to indulgence which could affect them through their generative organs. For the female, menstrual cramps can sometimes be quite severe.

5-4-9

Bert Betty Ed Bess Louise Les Tess Reid Brigitte Filbert Lyle

Putting their best foot forward is quite an easy task for these people. Unfortunately, their other foot can cripple them. This duality is rather interesting: their higher side is motivated by compassion and love for others and with kindness and generosity; their other side is an uncontrollable intensity that can flare up and inflame their emotions to a fever pitch. To control these extremes in their emotional nature is quite difficult. It will either express outwardly as temper or inwardly as an extreme frustration.

There is no doubt about their cleverness and their quick minds. When they are on someone's side, they are loving and supportive; as opponents they are formidable. They have an impulsive nature: their skepticism can be aroused on an impulse and color their thinking. Their tendency is to prejudge on the basis of their strong feelings that have been aroused impulsively.

At times they can receive an impression of a situation that is absolutely accurate because of their level of intuition. However, the truth of their impressions depends upon the state of their emotions. If they are predisposed to certain ideas, then that of course becomes the basis for their judgement. The trouble with this quality is their changing moods, and the nature of that mood is what determines whether the thought impulse comes from a true or imaginary source.

They draw from an idealism and a desire to serve life in some humanitarian capacity. Suffering moves them to respond through compassion and an urge to do something to alleviate the problem. When they are motivated by their greater idealism and a noble cause, they can awaken a passion that is beautiful to see. Their fierce drive and intense feelings can tend towards fanaticism if they are not careful. If the rest of their make-up compounds their emotional intensity, then such things as their religious orientation can be taken to extremes.

Not only do they have a compassion for people, but their love-making can be fraught with an unbridled passion. This all represents the tremendous emotion of this influence and the difficulty in understanding and channeling this power. At the heart of it is their undying search for truth.

They cannot rest unless their life has a greater meaning and direction to it. If their life turns towards indulgence or they turn against everything, then they develop real problems. Self-pity being their devil, they can pursue trouble with a vengeance, and then they become their own worst enemy.

The cause of truth and justice for all is a very strong motivation in their life. An injustice registers in their solar plexus life a knife stab, and then justice must be served. Others may let a little injustice go but not these types. Unfortunately, their feelings become quite intense and their confrontations will always betray their anger.

If through their birth date, they are passive types, then the inward repression and frustration will cause them to avoid getting involved for fear of their own outbursts and the guilt of hurting someone.

Their emotional intensity affects their nervous systems.

5-5-1

Gerry Perry Edith Emily Gilbert Errin Edwin Greg Mitchell Shen Philippe Aruna Becky Shauna

There are few people so fiercely independent as these types. When they put their minds to a task, nothing can stop them, as long as they are left alone to pursue it without any interference from others. As children they are strong-willed, physical, and not easy to discipline. If their time of birth lends itself to this strong individualistic name, they can be extremely creative. If their true nature through their birth date is social, then much of their lives will be frustrated because of the extreme independence of their name.

As these people mature they discover that they are quite different from all others. They are antisocial and inwardly rebel and refuse to follow traditional paths. They quickly discover the pointless exercise of the daily ritual carried out by the mass of people. Finding their own way becomes their lifelong quest. Working for or with others is difficult.

Freedom is a key word or idea in their mind. They are motivated by the impulse to change the world in some way or be rid of it by escaping into their own world where they can do their own thing. They unconsciously respond to injustice with the urge to fight. Truth is their first priority and they are unforgiving when they have been dealt an unfair blow. They must be careful not to get caught up in their anger and lose the fight because of the urge to get even. If their motivation is right and true, they can move mountains.

They are intense, restless, and inquisitive about everything. If developed, their creative potential has no bounds. Their ingenuity will always express through an aspect of originality that will be colored by their intensity.

If they do not develop their creativity, this dynamic and intense force will manifest as a frustration which they will turn against themselves. They totally lack a sense of humor.

With these names they are destined to a rather lonely life. Working out relationships is an almost impossible task for them.

They see others' faults quickly and can be quite candid, letting people know how they see them. They do not have a way with words. It is their lesson to right the wrongs of humanity, but they must learn to do it from a point of wisdom rather than from an impulsive or emotional reaction to somebody's faults. If they cannot learn this, they usually dismiss people and seek a life away from others.

These people need a sense of purpose in order to channel their energy. If this is the case, their natural sense of perseverance and endurance can almost see them do the impossible, especially when they are motivated by a cause or a search for truth.

They must be cautious of too much introspection where they become prey to vagrant and negative thought forms. Their love of wide open spaces and the challenge of the ski slopes, or anything that provides a challenge, is a natural outlet for them.

They usually have a rugged physical disposition but are prone to bouts of depression and stomach ulcers. If they have an accident, it is their head or extremities that suffer.

5-6-2

Ted Mike Dennis Rex Mildred Kelly Penny Bridget Sydney Brett Fredrick Nigel Myles Glen Winnie Muhammad Sylvie

These people are quick-minded, clever, with a gift-of-the-gab, and rather impressionable. Their aim is to please others for the sake of retaining their friendships. In other words, peace at all costs becomes their imperative. Sometimes this will lead to wrong decisions to save face or usually to no decision because it seems the safest course.

They are the perfect diplomats, always trying to please both sides but sometimes sacrificing their own ideas in order to avoid confrontations or issues. Although they can be very clever, they must be aware of talking themselves into a corner. These people possess a fluidity of speech that is quite remarkable; in the extreme, it becomes a fault, and their undoing.

They have charm and a friendliness that is very disarming. Their greatest challenge is to follow through with their promises. They have the best intentions but suffer from procrastination. To avoid hurt feelings, their own or others, they avoid issues, confrontations and quick decisions. They have answers for everything on all occasions and are masters at delaying and beating around the bush.

It is through people that they get ahead, from their cleverness and not necessarily from hard work. If they have not had a good upbringing, their submissive and impressionable natures can lead them into all sorts of indulgences and influences from associating with the wrong crowd. This is so because they have a daring to try new things when influenced by others. On their own, they would not dare.

On the positive side, they can offer good counsel or advice because of their intuitive natures. They know exactly where others are coming from, how they feel, and what they need to hear. Law could be their specialty because they know exactly what to say and how to say it. Sales is natural for them because of their gentle approach, although they would rather have people come to them because they do not take too easily to rejection. Direct sales is too hard on them. They have versatility and ingenuity but lack the confidence to stand on their own. Their quickness of mind makes them intelligent and perceptive; if misdirected they can become clever operators.

They must learn to discriminate between truth and fiction, otherwise their tendency to bend the truth can become habitual and unconscious. They must not be deceived by their own cleverness.

They work well with others and thrive on encouragement, but if they once become influenced by life in the fast lane, they can become somewhat unreliable in their work and in their relationships because they are easily influenced by deals and ways of making an easy buck.

If these names are not carefully balanced with a surname, they can suffer from all the negative elements mentioned as well as indulgence in rich and sweet foods which will affect them mainly in the kidney area and the stomach.

5-7-3

Ben Ken Reg Mel Sherry
Levi Cecily Chen

All things lie in the balance; any quality of character that expresses to the extreme upsets the whole. With these names there is a quickness of mind, a restlessness, a drive and an impulsive element that undermines the overall stability.

If there is an early direction and discipline in their lives, they could accomplish extraordinary things. However, this is not usually the case with these people. Initially they are motivated with the impulse to create and achieve, but their biggest problem is in following through. Inspiration may initiate action, but when patience and perseverance are called for, they easily become bored and further fields always look a lot greener.

Their quickness of mind makes them perceptive and able to learn things quickly, provided it is in the realm of their natural interests. They are inventive and original.

In relationships they have a difficult time because of an intolerance towards those who are not as clever as they are. Their impulsive retort to others' ideas soon gives them the reputation of being skeptical and argumentative. Their urge for self-expression over-rides their ability to listen closely to what others have to say.

When we first meet these types, they give the impression of being gregarious, fun and lively people. Only later do we discover their great need for independence. They do not work well for or with others. Freedom would be a word that describes their primary need.

Travel, change, and a new challenge is their basic requirement or boredom and an intensity in the area of the solar plexus could cause them to experience some very self-destructive moments in their lives. This would be particularly true if their birth date inclines them to a more stable life purpose.

Any occupation that relates to sales, promotion, or a great deal of variety will appeal to them and can then keep them on the straight and narrow. In these situations they can be dynamic and creative.

They are confident and determined when they live for a cause, but watch out when things go awry. They can become fuming mad whenever there is an injustice. Then they will fight with whatever means is at their disposal. It is their purpose to discover a truth in the midst of the battle, but in the heat of the fight their emotions usually take over and the motive is lost through a blind urge to get even.

If they could ever stay on track, their versatility could see them accomplish on the level of people like

Ben Franklin. Otherwise the frustration of this power unexpressed can lead to some terrible moods of depression and indulgence.

Their mind and thoughts sometimes work faster than their speech and cause them to slur their words. They could be masters at debate but must discover the difference between a friendly dialogue and argument.

If there is sufficient balance in the rest of their make-up, they could achieve on many levels except one—relaxation and peace of mind will tend to be just beyond their reach. They are rolling stones that gather no moss.

Their stomachs and liver can be their weak spot if they indulge in their appetites. They should never drink alcohol.

5-8-4

Jerry Percy Sidney Clyde Neil
Monique Miles Billie Lew Merv

These people demonstrate practicality, inventiveness, and a strong need to do things their own way. There is a dual influence here that inevitably gnaws at their stomach and intestinal tract. On one hand, all they want is a stable job and home life; but, they can never understand why they mentally respond with dissatisfaction to so much that goes on in their life. This duality combines a restlessness and a desire for stability.

These two elements are quite incompatible. The result is an intensity that affects their relationships and their health. When they are at their best, they are creative and can fix almost anything. They have the patience and concentration that allows them to explore and invent new ways of doing things.

Their strength is in their potential for research. They lean towards mechanics and machinery or anything dealing with the practical and material world. Working away by themselves is what makes them happy. They are good with figures and their minds are very logical.

This influence is rather materialistic and closed to

the more philosophical aspects of life. Their skepticism and resistance to theory and idealism limits their circle of friends to those who, like themselves, deal with those things that come within the range of the five senses. In fact, they can be quite antisocial when they are pushed the wrong way.

An injustice can rankle and eat away at their insides much longer than it should. They will think about the injustice, but because of a lack of confidence and the fear of confrontation, they will harbor their feelings until they get sick. Changing their workplace is an option that they would first consider before they would confront the issues that bother them.

They are reliable and hard working and meticulous in their approach to their work. Once they set their minds to a task, nothing will deter them from seeing it through to the end. No matter what the obstacle, they have perseverance and endurance and a way of finding the missing pieces to a difficult job.

If their path through the birth date is inspirational, then this becomes quite a difficult quality to handle. Because it is so practical and restless, their efforts in life are usually short-lived. Their interest in a job or project lasts only for so long and then they feel the urge to move on. This is always the problem when our personalities through our names are either too practical or too inspirational and where it is contrary to the inner or true nature.

They have a strong drive to achieve but tend to fail to climb the ladder of success. In their efforts they often end up doing the dirty work or the work that nobody else wants to do. They are not organizers or leaders, and always find themselves picking up after others. Fixing and repairing is their lot in life, whether it is on a mechanical or a business level.

5-9-5

Terry Cecil Ned Enid Maureen Brent Kent Trent Leigh Kerry Derrick Jenny Drew Whitney Juliana

These people are quick-minded, clever, gutsy, ambitious, and quite restless. Their versatility enables them to accomplish almost anything they put their minds to. They cannot tolerate injustice of any kind and will fight to uphold a truth. They live for the cause of truth and are quite reactive when they are repressed or thwarted in any way. This is a very dynamic and intense quality. They must have a direction or this intensity will produce so much frustration and chaos that their lives will become impossible to live.

They are natural promoters and salespeople that will not take "no" for an answer. Life has little meaning to them if there is no challenge. They will pursue an interest as long as the challenge remains but will move on as soon as the challenge turns to routine and boredom. They cannot see that real growth is achieved through building block upon block. To them, further fields always look greener, and a change looks far more exciting than the stability that comes from consistent effort and following things through to completion.

Their lives are a series of experiences with a great deal learned at a cost; however, the one thing that usually eludes them is happiness and peace of mind. They can never relax, except for short periods of time and usually only after some great physical exertion.

They are versatile and their love of freedom is the essence of their being. Their fierce independence and restlessness make it difficult for them in relationships. At times they can be quite critical and know just what to say that hurts, but they find it very hard to take criticism themselves.

When focused they can achieve almost the impossible. They have an insatiable urge for discovery and new things. They love the idea of change and travel.

They can be disruptive and radical in their outlook on life and respond from the gut level to anything that smacks of an untruth. There is nothing they won't try, once their interest is awakened. They have a touch of the daredevil and could become great gamblers.

They are driven by their intensity to succeed, but when depressed, they are prey to some very destructive thoughts towards themselves. They never forget a slight against themselves and must curb the urge to get even.

Their weakness lies in their solar plexus and their stomach. They are prone to ulcers and other stomach upsets. Tension will also affect them in the muscles around the shoulders and neck.

Sleep can be impossible when they become worked up mentally.

When these people are motivated by a cause of justice or truth, they can move mountains. It is their purpose to use their mind and intellect to sift through the old outworn dogmas and to uncover the truths of life that others lack the courage to take on.

6-1-7

Walter Harvey Warren Anne Grace Hazel Frieda Terence Todd Simon Stewart Mathew Cory Darrell Blaine Pearl Alexis Ashley Katelyn Corbin Thea Francine Glenda Harriet

This is a quiet, refined, studious, serious, and very responsible quality. Nothing gets past these people. They could be very intellectual if their sensitivity and lack of expression does not cause them to become too reclusive. They have a deep love of nature and a strong artistic leaning.

Their love of learning and books gives them a good grasp of life, but they might fail to convince others of their ideas because of a restriction in their verbal expression. Writing is something that they need to develop and use to clarify and to express their ideas, otherwise they can suffer a great deal of misunderstanding. They feel deeply about things and must create an outlet for this depth through music, art, and writing or they will begin to doubt their own abilities.

Here is a quality that is so responsible and serious that if they are not careful, they can worry to the point of distraction.

Life and its mystery holds a great fascination for them. They are naturally philosophical or religious with a deep yearning for peace and tranquillity. Nothing moves them so much as the rising moon coming over the mountain or the setting sun going down into the sea. They are romantics who dream of a better day and a better life away from the confusion of the marketplace.

These people perceive more than most, either through their emotional sensitivity or because of a developed intellect. This can make life a little difficult for them because they see the flaws in others and tend to become quite judgmental. It is difficult for them to be tolerant of others. They will either point out others' faults or go into a mood of silence and refuse to communicate. Unconsciously this is their way of getting even. Of course this is their own undoing.

If they can grow intellectually and move away from their moods and their reclusive tendencies, these people can excel as writers and teachers of philosophy. They have concentration and the ability to think deeply into any subject of interest to them. This is a quality of the mind with a profound potential for insight, if it can distinguish between worry and creative thought. If they do not master worry and lapse into a world of dreams and fantasy, they can become influenced through mysticism and unreality as an escape from the crass world of materiality.

These people have imagination and a profound appreciation for flowers, art, music, and good literature. They have usually read more books than most people because of their deep interest in life and its mysteries.

They are very independent and must never work for others or they will be stifled. Small talk is beneath them. Their verbal expression is usually restricted to the deeper aspects of life. They are uncomfortable in crowds and usually have little to say unless the atmosphere is safe and friendly. At times fluid speech and the right words simply abandon them and they retreat into embarrassment and silence.

Their weakness lies in excessive worry and susceptibility to heart, lung and bronchial problems with a shortness of breath.

6-2-8

**Floyd Allen Ross Colin Gretta Marge
Glenna Leah Brenda Jenna Alyse
Jasmine Kendra Terra Bernard Casey
Hartley Lance Braden Janine Eliza
Velma Edgar Bettina Rollin**

These people are very fortunate in having a name that gives positivity, self-confidence, and a naturally clear perspective of the difference between right and wrong. They possess a great deal of common sense. Poise and mental objectivity are their natural traits.

They cannot easily be pulled into argument or emotional disputes. Their objectivity allows them to stand back and view life as separate from the confusion. Their minds are very analytical and fair in their reasoning. They are quietly dignified and know the lesson of discretion in holding back from saying things on impulse. They would make good judges because they are not swayed by emotional appeals.

Leadership and management are their natural forte and they quickly gravitate to positions of responsibility. Their ambition is to be on the top, either as the manager or in their own business. Banking and money hold a fascination for them. The need to establish financial independence is very strong.

Their understanding of people makes them excellent organizers, with the self-assurance to take charge of any situation. If the rest of their make-up is unbalanced, they could become a little pushy; otherwise, they are usually quite modest about their own strengths.

Being very ambitious, they work hard for the things they want out of life. Their wealth complex gives them an excellent taste for the good things of life, from a material standpoint. They buy the best without being ostentatious.

They are quick and insightful when making decisions regarding investments and spending large sums of money. They are not gamblers. There is a shrewdness in their nature that comes from knowing, almost as if it arises from a sixth sense. Their mind works logically and is always focused on success, therefore their confidence assures opportunities.

In becoming successful, they should be aware of the spiritual aspect of their life. Their power to accumulate and to build should be motivated by an ideal to contribute to life for the sake of others. Spirit, being a passion for life, can only be awakened when there is a noble purpose motivating us. These people can become preoccupied with merely acquiring and possessing and then they lose their humanity.

Normally they are not overly materialistic. Family

and friends mean a great deal to them. They are always aware of what is going on around them politically and otherwise. Being very worldly they have opinions about everything without being opinionated. Working in the community gives them the chance to learn their skills of organizing others. This is their power. Helping to delegate and organize makes them aware of their tremendous ability to influence others. Leadership is one of the most rewarding positions to aspire to, and, of course, brings a great responsibility with it. These people are authority figures who must earn the right to their power over others, or suffer the consequences of the abuse of power.

In a woman this quality is sometimes a little too masculine and tends to make her quite competitive where she loses the naturally soft feminine influence. Any imbalance affects these people through generative disorders.

6-3-9

**Earl Keath Lea Sheila Brown Harvie
Jody Holly Erica Matthew Bailey
Carmen Carrie Gena Jessa Lori Elijah
Reece Tylor Hailley**

The only potential weakness in these names is their tendency to be a little too emotional. If their energies and time are spent in cultivating their artistic talents, then their beauty can shine forth,

These people radiate love from their eyes. They respond to kindness with warmth and gratitude. Giving to others is their natural way. Their hearts respond with compassion whenever they see suffering. They are meant to administer to the needy and to inspire people with their love. This can be done either through the medium of music or through some humanitarian endeavor.

If they lack direction or self-discipline, then their lives can be difficult. In that case the emotion builds up as a craving for love and sex, accompanied by feelings of self-pity.

From early in their lives they desire to perform some meaningful work. They cannot do mundane or mediocre work without suffering. This is both an intelligent and an idealistic quality that is strongly motivated by a humanitarian urge. They are inspired when they are motivating others through their love, and terribly depressed when there is no meaning to their work.

In the performing arts, they can move people to tears because of the depth of their emotion; and similarly, their own tears flow quickly and spontaneously when faced with the suffering of animals, people or situations where there is a loss of love.

They are very responsible and take seriously all their commitments. As caregivers they excel. Their love has a sincerity to it that is healing in itself. They feel the problems or sickness of others and their sympathy is genuine. Their challenge is not merely to be sympathetic but to help through wisdom or suffer the consequences of being drawn into and influenced by others' problems.

Their compassion is the ultimate of human sentiment and must be directed by their intelligence. As teachers, they could be inspired if they understand that the spoken word releases the greatest power of all when it is empowered by compassion and the wisdom of life. Their difficulty lies in not being able to cut through the problematic area of those they are helping and not being able to distinguish between sympathy to the problem and sympathy with the very soul of another individual.

It is hard not to fall in love with these people because they are so loving. Love is their greatest asset

as well as their greatest liability. If there is not sufficient balance in the rest of their names, they tend to
live for love rather than love to live and give. It is in
their giving that they discover the true essence of
love. If they have not realized this, then they are forever seeking a lover to satisfy a spiritual impulse.
When they have discovered the universality of love,
they will never again suffer the loss of it or the insatiable craving for it. It is merely a matter of perspective.

These people have a great potential for creativity
and accomplishment because of their confidence
and strong responsible natures, if directed toward
meaningful pursuits; otherwise they can become
complainers and worry over trifles.

A constant fear of loss and self-pity can lead to nervous exhaustion and breakdown.

6-4-1

Lois Bob Katie Mae Vera Boyd Eva Agnes Alfred Kody Marie Camille Tessa Clifford Edward Elias Damien Stacey Faye Elsa Rod

Intelligent and outspoken would sum up the character of these people. They are independent and self-confident. If their entire name is balanced they set their own course early in life and can achieve a great deal. In the case where they are not totally balanced and their need for independence is curtailed, they can become pushy, stubborn and antisocial, otherwise this is quite a positive and creative influence.

The main characteristic in these names is their natural mental perception of life. There is a logic here and a practicality. They are not always conscious that they know more than most others until they rise up into positions of responsibility, then they begin to realize that others may rise by the force of their personalities and not by the force of reason. This influence is quite intellectual with a great deal of common sense.

As they achieve a certain autonomy, their creative talents flourish. They are natural pioneers of new ways and original ideas. If circumstances find them in supportive roles, they can be quite frustrated. Their determination and perseverance can see them through almost any obstacle.

While they are reasonably social types, their candid verbal expression can produce adverse reactions in others because they do not have a fluid verbal ability. Their speech is straight to the point and honest. At times they can be at a loss for words and feel awkward and then desire to be alone. They can stumble over their words due to an uneasy rapport with certain types. They need to be with people who can take and exchange ideas with the same open and candid manner.

Their strong sense of responsibility and commitment to their tasks makes them perennial thinkers. They function on the side of reason and are always thinking about the rights and wrongs of things. Their paternal or maternal instincts make them good parents, as well as giving them a feeling for what is going on in the community.

While this deep sense of responsibility compels them to be thinking all the time, their downfall could be their inability to distinguish between creative thought and worry. If they tend towards worry, they can interfere in their children's and others' lives because they think they know best; their lack of control over this negative habit can cause alienation of those they love. This bossy quality arises out of their deep concern for others. The extent to which they have achieved their true role as entrepreneurs will determine how much they are plagued by this negative side. They can learn not to be bossy as they climb the ladder of personal success towards a point of true self-confidence. Potentially they are leaders and teachers and desire to be looked upon as authority figures because of their keen minds and their interest in acquiring knowledge. Of course they must earn the right to respect.

This is usually quite a healthy and robust quality; any tension or undue worry would affect them in the senses of the head.

6-5-2

John Collin Morris Nadine Andrew Charlie Dianne Dayle Rock Desiree Renee Paige Elissa Jade Jamie Jodi Rachel Robyn Byron Gerald Shane Tony Stefan Cody Timothy

These people possess a lovely quality. They are soft, gentle, and intelligent types normally. Their minds are perceptive with common sense values. If the rest of their make-up is not strong and balanced, then the only drawback to this influence is their procrastinating nature.

This quality lends itself to diplomacy and tact. The intuitive element in these people allows them to feel and respond to others with understanding and concern. Making peace with others is always uppermost in their minds; they cannot live in discord with others. They are very impressionable to the thoughts and feelings of people and must, therefore, learn to understand the heart and mind of their fellow man in order to become the peacemakers of life.

They are quick-minded with a fluid verbal expression. Their thoughts appear and are expressed with a spontaneity that could surprise even themselves. Becoming overly expressive could be a problem and indulgence in small talk or gossip must be controlled.

Their intellect is keen and sharp with a natural ability to perceive the difference between truth and fiction.

They have a serious and responsible nature but lack initiative and drive. Invariably they work for others which could be a source of aggravation in their lives if they are meant to express themselves as leaders or if they desire to run their own business. If they do go into business, they look for partners with that supportive influence. Since they lack confidence, their success is achieved by utilizing their clever minds through education and their natural ability to work with others.

Getting their hands dirty or having to do manual labor is out of character for them. They would rather sit and enjoy the company of others, utilizing their communication skills.

These people feel more comfortable in the company of the opposite sex. This is an idealistic and romantic quality. On the dance floor they move in perfect harmony with their partner. Their intuitive natures allow them to blend easily with whomever they accompany. They are graceful and diplomatic.

Standing up for themselves could be difficult at times because they so easily register the feelings and discomfort of others and therefore tend to avoid potentially embarrassing situations. They will never take sides in a dispute. Their higher nature should express as a peacemaker because of their natural ability to see both sides of a situation. Their nurturing ability makes them natural counselors and teachers.

If there is too much imbalance in the rest of their make-up, they will suffer from lack of confidence leading to procrastination, laziness, and a tendency to bend the truth, which could give them the reputation of being great talkers but slow in producing the goods.

Normally this is quite a healthy quality, with a susceptibility to kidney ailments and excessive worry.

6-6-3

Charles James Jane Jean Alice Maxine Tom Frances Stacie Bethany Amber Angel Bobbi Candice Claire Jackie Isabel Jessica Meghan Alec Dillon Jon Sean Tyson Layne Bronwyn

These names awaken self-expression and intelligence. They usually only succeed in life if they enter into the artistic world as actors, musicians, or into fields of endeavor where they are teaching and inspiring an audience. If they end up in routine office jobs, their lives reach a dead end, then the negative side expresses through intolerance, argument, and an endless series of complaints.

Because of a quick mind and fluid verbal expression, their debating abilities are excellent, provided they learn the difference between debate and argument. They are usually far ahead of anyone else and have a quick retort to others' thoughts. Sometimes their spontaneity and love of speaking make them poor listeners. In debates they must have the last word, and this can create problems in their relationships.

They love to be in the center of the crowd or in the spot light. They have wit, confidence, and charm.

Their entertaining manner endears them to all people. When they are involved in such things as acting or speaking, their imaginations work in a profoundly creative way. They are natural and easy with all types of people.

There is a strong love nature at the core of their personality. They must learn to express it wisely or be pulled into situations that can lead them into trouble. They are easily drawn to the opposite sex and delight in their company. Love inspires them and actually serves as the strongest motivation in their lives. Consequently, their challenge is to understand the lower and the higher aspects of the power of love.

They seem to know a great deal about almost everything and have an opinion for as many things. Following up on their thoughts and ideas is not a strong point. This is why they must work in a field that inspires them, otherwise boredom destroys their initiative. They are so clever that they could mistakenly believe that knowing about things could take the place of action and accomplishment. Unless they have discipline, their efforts are scattered.

Being such an emotional and clever quality, they can be extremely creative when they are directed in a positive way; but, if the rest of their names are unbalanced, this can turn out to be a rather self-indulgent influence. This is reminiscent of the teacher's note to the parent, "Your child does not live up to his potential."

These people know the value and importance of play. Sometimes they could be accused of not taking life seriously enough. Their happy-go-lucky natures keep them young, provided they do not take to alcohol.

Their keen intellect and clear mental perception can bring out an intolerance for those who are mentally slower than themselves. These names produce a quality that is like walking on the thin edge between extreme creativity and emotional indulgence. They could go either way depending on their early discipline or lack of it.

Their weakness could be laziness and an inclination toward extremes. Any tension would then affect them in the liver.

6-7-4

Roy Dale Karen Elma Elva Robin Albert Darcie Fraser Helene Megan Melinda Toni Blake Bradley Brendan Brock Dominic Kaleb Rory

We owe the work of science, technology, mathematics, and form to these people. They are not afraid of hard work, detail, or routines that would test another's patience to the limit. They have an eye for perfection and precision. Being involved in the most patient, detailed, and absorbing jobs can be an inspiration to these types, while it is totally boring to the more artistic temperament.

There is no shortage in their minds of concentration and attention to detail. With this quality, work can always be looked upon as a source of interest. They adapt well to all kinds of work. They are reliable, honest, and very responsible.

Mechanics, mathematics, accounting, computers, or if we can imagine, just plain housework, can be a pure joy. Through their concentration, they make new discoveries in their chosen field. Their perseverance and endurance see them through to the end of their projects. Around the home they love to putter and repair and see that everything is in order. They love their home and family. Change and a disruption of their routine can be upsetting to them.

The highest aspect of these names expresses through intellectual pursuits dealing with science and mathematics. They are fascinated by the workings of things. Their focus and attention to detail could be expressed in the study of the human mind itself and the psychology of the human condition. Their intellect knows no bounds when they become absorbed in the enquiry of life and form.

Research and its demand for painstaking detail inspires them to continue until enough pieces of information are gathered to form a complete picture.

Generally speaking, these names are quite balanced by themselves, but if the surnames and birth date do not balance, the negative aspects will manifest. When that is the case, they can become fussy and lost in the little things "... not being able to see the forest for the trees."

This is a quality that lives by facts and by that which comes within the realm of the five senses. If they are unbalanced, then their skepticism can close them to the more aesthetic values of life, and they can become lost in material pursuits exclusively. They could putter their whole lives away in meaningless hobbies that add up to much less than they expected in life.

They are traditionalists who do not change until the world view changes. They are inventive in science but not usually in religious or philosophical matters unless, of course, there is an overall balance, then their intellect could embrace religion as well.

They make good mothers and fathers as well as good homemakers. Their confidence is limited to those things that they are familiar with, and they do not dare to step into new fields without a thorough investigation. They could find working for others confining but lack the confidence to strike out on their own.

These are quite good names, but where there is imbalance, they can suffer in the intestinal tract through constipation and any ensuing problems.

6-8-5

**Wayne Lloyd Thelma Joy Molly Dolly
Dave Janet Scott Tommy Courtenay
Emma Lena Benjamin Brennan
Davinder Gareth Johnny Jory Lane
Neal Bjorn Eileen**

Unless there is imbalance in the rest of their make-up, these people are intelligent and as clever as the best of them. They are quick-minded and able to perceive the flaws in others' concepts. Their minds scrutinize everything. It is the truth that is their motivating force.

They are free spirits who find themselves going contrary to almost everything and everyone else. If they are repressed in any way, they can become rebellious or self-indulgent and create chaos in their environments. These types can accomplish ten times more than anyone else because of their drive and fearlessness. They dare to be great and dare anyone who tries to stop them. If this force is not disciplined and directed, the frustrations can lead to self-destruction because of the inherent mental intensity.

This influence contains a profound mental capacity for analysis and deduction, always stimulated by their response to untruth. They are here to right the wrongs of humanity. Restlessness and change are integral parts of their lives. If there is no challenge in their work, change is impending. They work for and demand their independence. Their minds never stop cogitating about things. They are serious and worrisome and spend many sleepless nights playing the same mental tunes.

Their accomplishments, unfortunately, may not include the ability to find peace of mind. Only when their lives are motivated by a noble purpose or cause can they begin to feel a deep satisfaction in their work and in their life, otherwise they search endlessly for the elusive answer to life and their miseries. They will travel the world either literally or through books and learning to satisfy their insatiable desire for answers to their questions. They must understand the force that drives them or they will be driven to distraction.

Their creative impulse does not conceive any limitations when awakened. They draw from an energy that seems unlimited but definitely has its limitations when they push themselves too hard. Their deep sense of responsibility and commitment can drive them to a point of exhaustion, which may induce a kind of relaxation that serves as a temporary relief from their worries.

This is a very mental or intellectual force that has a tremendous insight into things as long as it flows out of the strength of their independence. If they are thwarted in their efforts, their minds can become quite critical and their skepticism can blind them to the truth. Injustice can make them mad, and they are formidable fighters. They must learn the great truth: that answers come in the midst of the battle only when the fight becomes impersonal. It is truth that must be the focus and not getting even. If this influence is misdirected, the repression experienced will self-destruct in some form of indulgence.

Worry is their nemesis. They would do well to laugh more often. Their criticism of others can become quite intense and holding grudges could be a problem. Holding on to their problems mentally invariably leads to ulcers or other stomach problems.

6-9-6

**Alex Rae Harley Greta Stella Mabel
Janice Diane Cecilia Ashleigh Celeste
Edna Melissa Haley Maggie Shelagh
Andre Brayden Troy Wade Victor
Clinton Dean Darren Evan Kory
Michael Shea Stanley Garret Helga**

Responsibility is the key here. These people have a strong maternal or paternal nature which expresses through parenthood, teaching, or nurturing others in some way. They must always be in a position of responsibility, otherwise they will never be happy. As leaders in the community or in their own business, they find their self-worth. This is a quality of strength and individuality with a great intellectual capacity.

They take great pride in doing things on their own initiative. This is a quality that would never admit they do not know something. Even as children they can be heard saying "I know." It is beneath them to be found not knowing. It is their purpose to instruct others without becoming too bossy or interfering. This is a know-it-all quality on the negative side, but generally speaking they have a keen sense of knowing and comprehending the difference between truth and fiction.

If there is too much imbalance, they can become possessive and overbearing and prevent their children from trying things on their own and in their own way. They tend to know best but must cultivate a way of instructing that does not interfere with another person's natural way. This negative element occurs if there is any imbalance and if they are frustrated by not being recognized as the authority. If their imbalance finds them in a subordinate role, then the bossy side of their nature will emerge.

No one can assume responsibility as well as these people. They naturally gravitate into positions where they can be in charge and helpful, instructing others in the way of things.

This is a very mental quality that tends to worry excessively when things go wrong and, therefore, must learn the great lesson of not crossing their bridges before getting to them. This represents the challenge of having confidence in our inner consciousness. The future is not for us to know but to work out day by day.

They love children and are good disciplinarians. This parenting instinct lies at the heart of these people. Nothing satisfies them more than having people come to them for their knowledge, expertise, and advice. They are not particularly sympathetic to others' problems but are very encouraging and helpful when they see them striving for success.

Self-confidence, practicality, and a logical mind

can take these people a long way in life. They have the ability to rise up the ladder in their ambitions and to succeed at anything they attempt. They learn quickly because they love knowledge, and they quickly move in to take charge when others wait to be asked.

Their versatility and wide range of knowledge make them good conversationalists and eager to help wherever they can, particularly if they can be the boss.

These people are quite healthy and the only weakness lies in their tendency to worry too much if the rest of their make-up is not balanced.

7-1-8

Olga Gloria Rosa Jordan Mason Noreen Asmena Natalie Carmela Josiah Antony Aretha Sondra

Deep, quiet, efficient, and business-like are the strong points of these people. They are completely reliable and responsible types. When something needs to be done, they will quietly do the job; they do not have to be asked.

They could be excellent leaders because of their organizational skills. Their sensitivity would make them very aware of other people's feelings. Sometimes they will just do a job themselves rather than direct others to do it for fear of hurting another's feelings.

They are profoundly aware of everything that is going on in their working environment. They could be running the show in such an unassuming way that the less wary would not be conscious of their influence and power. Those who do not see or understand their proficiency may not take them seriously. These people are the strong and silent types who are seldom given the credit they deserve.

Their refinement and appreciation of material values usually shows in the clothes they wear, although there is nothing showy about these people.

Their homes are usually works of art. They have a love for beauty, art, and literature, with a natural skill for decoration and design. One should never underestimate the potential of these types, nor should they underestimate their own capacities. Their sensitive side draws them into nature and environments where there is refinement and beauty.

In a crowd one would not usually notice them. They are not naturally sociable unless the mood is respectful and philosophical. Coarse language and noise are very disturbing to them. One will never find them arguing a point because that is beneath them. They will just become quiet and dismiss the issue from their minds.

They are strongly independent and capable of managing their own affairs. If a woman with this name is pushed around in a relationship, she will usually end up on her own and then can become unduly independent.

This is a quality that lacks the ability to demonstrate feelings outwardly but still craves to be understood without knowing how to be open to it. In their personal lives, they can suffer from misunderstandings. The first sign of being misunderstood is a cool, unapproachable silence. Their verbal expression vanishes when they are under pressure or nervous about anything.

At times, they can be cold and shrewd in their business dealings. They can recognize an opportunity and move to take advantage while others are still talking about it. They need to be their own boss or in a situation where they are an authority.

They are fair and just in all their dealings. Their minds think objectively because they are not swayed by emotion.

This quality can suffer through generative disorders, as well as problems affecting the heart, lungs and bronchial organs.

7-2-9

Raymond Glynn Angelina Fiona Clayton Margo Nicola Vanessa Nicholas Sebastian Samson Konrad Charmaine

While sensitivity is a wonderful aspect of the human mind, these names possess a little too much. At times these people experience feelings that are profound. They are moved to tears very easily over their experiences in life.

While love inspires them to heights of grandeur, losses in their affections can drag them into the depths of despair. Their imaginations can transport them into realms of fantasy where it is difficult to separate truth from fiction. It is easy for these people to be carried away by their emotions because of this profound sensitivity.

In theory, life is very simple. It only requires that we control our thoughts and become masters of our destiny. With these people, the emotions tend to take over. A mood becomes all absorbing. A slight can grow out of proportion. In other words, negative feelings are difficult to shake off.

These types are finely tuned to elements of mysticism. We must all be awakened to the mystery of life to some degree. With these people, life in the material world is too difficult, which usually turns them to seek religious or philosophical paths, with a tendency towards the occult—wherein lie great truths along with a graveyard of non-truths. Only when there is balance between the two natures within an individual can the mind perceive the hidden truths in life and religion, otherwise it is easy to be carried away and become a victim of theories that appeal to one's sense of mysticism.

It is not easy for these people to use their powers of analysis without being influenced by their emotions. They must realize that religion, like science, is governed by truths perceived or not perceived, and progress takes place only on the basis of actual truth or law. Because they feel so deeply, they can delude themselves into believing something is true merely because it feels so good.

In the highest sense, these types are meant to be the spiritual teachers of the race; but, like all of us, they must learn the practical side of life, and that is very difficult for them. They are naturally artistic and should find an outlet through the arts.

Through their feelings they are aware of the great beauty and meaning that lies in nature. The sun rising or setting can move them to tears. A good book or movie can touch them in ways that could never be shared. In fact, they soon learn that they are different and that nobody understands them. They should write their thoughts and plumb the depths of their psyche for the truths that can arise through their sensitivity.

Unfortunately, their lives are usually quite troubled and their preoccupation with their problems interferes with their potential creativity.

They live for love, but it could elude them forever, even though their capacity to give is endless. Their compassion for human suffering requires an outlet through humanitarian work. If they cannot express this part of their natures, then the negative aspect will manifest through self-pity and depression.

Their weakness lies in the chest and bronchial organs as well as the entire nervous system.

7-3-1

Allison Arnold Taylor Conrad Ronald Rhoda Monica Daniela Brynn Breanna Anton Jackson Arael Cora Marlon Pablo Roland

This influence is antisocial, independent, and strong-willed. If any of these people are social, as defined through the birthdate, then they will suffer from the longing for deep social contact. It is difficult for these types to understand what it means to be open and friendly. They cannot outwardly demonstrate affection, nor can they receive it. This is the typical lone-wolf, wandering through the woods alone and finding solace with nature. With time, their misunderstandings with people tend to make them solitary creatures.

They draw from an element of consciousness that tunes them deeply to beauty and tranquillity. Small talk and meaningless conversation bore them. It is not long before they begin to withdraw in consequence of the confusion and chaos which reign in our mad, competitive world.

The first thing that vanishes in their life when they are misunderstood is their desire to communicate. After a while, they have little to say about anything; in fact, sometimes when things must be said, it becomes very difficult to be coherent. In their own privacy with their books or personal interests, they feel more content—or out in nature where they can regain their energy.

If there is some degree of balance in the rest of their make-up, the strength of this quality can accomplish a great deal. They are strong and determined with great perseverance. When they know what they want, nothing can stop them. There is a creativity that arises out of their fierce independence.

They may not have a lot to say, but what they lack in conversation, they make up in action. When they do speak, it is usually straight to the point, candid, and without any frills. They are deep, with strong opinions that are expressed only with those that will understand. "Casting pearls before swine," should be a familiar quotation to them. They are positive, skeptical, and original in everything they undertake.

They could never work for anyone else.

This influence can be quite hard on children who need friends but soon learn that their friendships are short-lived. Being hurt, they become uncommunicative and moody and unconsciously chase people away from them. There are absolutely no social graces with these names.

After a day's work, their gardens and their homes become their sanctuary. It is through writing, music, or painting that they could show the depth of their feelings. They are deeply philosophical and finely tuned to a mystical element that is felt as they commune with nature.

In relationships they are awkward and difficult to live with. They see others' faults and can be quite judgmental. They are not tolerant and can be cold and aloof when they are misunderstood. It is only in an atmosphere of depth and philosophy that they can be drawn out. In their moods they can shut others out with a coldness that can deeply hurt, and they know it, but they cannot easily change. It is this profound depth that is both their strong point and their nemesis.

Through tension they will be affected through the heart, lungs, and bronchial organs.

7-4-2

Moira Oscar Nolan Margaret Dora Sonya Mario Ursula Josephine Lynn Noah Damon Omar Meara Rasheda

This is a deeply sensitive and impressionable quality. Theses names are easily influenced by their environment. Any kind of discord will affect them adversely. They have a deep yearning to be understood but repress it by accommodating others' needs in place of their own. Seldom do they reveal their deeper sentiments about life for fear of misunderstanding.

Their conversation is usually in support of others' ideas rather than their own as a diversion or cover-up for feelings that lie deep inside and are revealed to no one but their closest confidant. They have a quiet and pleasant manner that is easily hurt and offended by the loud or coarse ways of others. When offended, they can withdraw mentally and never show their disappointment.

This is a refined and poetic influence. They are dreamers who love to spend time alone with their books, pets and flowers. The world of business and commerce is not for them. Their soft, quiet, and easygoing disposition requires an environment of music, art and creativity. If disciplined they could excel as writers of poetry and prose, usually fiction. They are very good listeners and can divine the feelings and intentions of others; therefore, they can offer advice that others need to hear, although they would never say anything that could hurt.

Perseverance and hard work are not usually a strong part of their character, and they must beware of being a bit lazy and subject to bouts of procrastination. Because of their deep sensitivity, and their fear of being misunderstood, they must guard against becoming involved in shallow and meaningless conversation. This deep and private side to their nature should be cultivated and expressed along philosophical and intellectual avenues or they will be forever misunderstood.

Lacking confidence, they need encouragement, support and love, otherwise they find life a little too difficult. Men of this sensitivity are drawn to the opposite sex for the safety and understanding they do not receive from other men. As for women in love, they often draw the support of strong masculine types, who never understand the romantic and sensitive natures of these names.

They are extremely accommodating and find it difficult to say no, for fear of disappointing, or witnessing the hurt feelings of anyone. They will do almost anything to avoid issues or confrontations. Being so soft, if they are taken advantage of, they may fight back eventually, but it is very hard on them.

This is not a particularly healthy or robust influence, and they are quite susceptible to colds and viruses that are going around. Their physical weakness lies in the heart, lungs, and bronchial organs, as well as the kidneys. Inevitably they suffer from poor circulation, with cold hands and feet.

These people are idealistic, helpful and diplomatic types. Their love of nature, including animals, flowers, and the tranquillity of a quiet mill pond, is the setting they require to become the artists that they are.

7-5-3

George Sharon Nora Donna Pamela Wallace Kaela Marianne Rachael Aron Harrison Jerome Nathaniel Norman Tobias Jonah Dalton

These people are deeply sentimental, artistic, misunderstood, and subject to mood swings. This is an emotional quality with deep feelings for nature and for people. Sometimes they can be outgoing and the "life of the party," and the very next moment they become withdrawn and uncommunicative. It is this deep emotional nature that they find hard to control or even understand.

They are so sensitive and impressionable to misunderstandings and unkindness that even against their own will they can suddenly become moody and a bit judgmental. When misunderstood they need to withdraw and reflect about things in an atmosphere of peace and quiet. They must guard against remaining in a mood and holding things against others for periods of time that are unreasonable. When they are at their best, they can be charming, deep, and quite philosophical.

They need to awaken and cultivate their talents along lines of writing, music, painting, or other artistic avenues if they are to ever understand their deeper natures. Being so sensitive and emotional, there is a strong tendency to escape from their responsibilities into a life of dreaming and imagination where they cannot find the balance between practicality and idealism. If they lose their sense of reality they can become indulgent in their emotions and lose their motivation. It is not easy for them to discipline themselves when they become disenchanted about the world of materiality and the work place.

When they can combine the elements of sociability with their artistic abilities, they can experience great moments of inspiration.

They have a deep loving nature that knows no bounds when awakened, but when misunderstood they just close up and become almost impossible to draw out. This can occur in an instant, sometimes on a level that is unconscious, and they are never the wiser to understand what actually caused the change.

They can experience moments of great verbal fluidity and spontaneity only to discover that it suddenly disappears when there is any discord or change in their mood.

The combined emotion and deep sensitivity could make life difficult for these types. If there is sufficient balance in the rest of their make-up, then the artistic potential could be realized. If that is so, then they could delve deeply into the realms of philosophy by using their minds, otherwise they are drawn into the realms of emotion with its illusions of mysticism and expectations which are never realized.

At times they have moments of profound beauty when alone in nature. Their senses, particularly the sense of smell, can transport them into heavenly experiences. They can be inspired to great heights, yet they know full well the analogy of the pendulum: that as high as it swings one way, it is bound to move as far down or in the opposite direction. Emotional stability is difficult for them to maintain.

If there is too much imbalance they could suffer from skin problems, liver ailments, and a weakness in the heart, lungs, and bronchial organs.

7-6-4

Thomas Harold Joan Carol Angela Gabriella Sonia Candace Coral Daniella Jacob Meaghan Logan Lola Lorelei

Painstakingly detailed, proficient, and patient are these types. Concentration, orderliness, and a focus on the finer points of a job are their main characteristics. These people are the analysts, scientists, and workers who deal best with mathematics, computers, mechanics, or anything that requires attention to detail. They have the patience and the power to finish the things they start. Theirs is the life of steady, systematic, and slow progress. Change can be very disturbing because it upsets the routine. They live by routine.

This is a quality that lives by the adage, "show me, I'm from Missouri." Their minds work on the basis of fact and within the realm of the five senses. They are not particularly theoretical or open to philosophical speculations. Things have to have the stamp of approval by academia or the scientific community before they will accept and follow a train of thought. They must see and understand from the basis of their own experience before an idea will register in their consciousness as a truth.

These people are naturally skeptical and slow to change. They are traditionalists who will not question the status quo.

Their love of detail can awaken an ingenuity and patience that can see them accomplish things others would give up in frustration. It is this patient enquiry and seeing a job well done that is the source of their inspiration. Their minds are meticulous in covering all the details and putting things in exactly the right place. This is the quality of research and science with a profound aptitude for discovering a truth through mathematics and form.

Confidence is not their strong point. They are afraid to step out and try something new. Familiar ways are the safest path for them. They are reliable and hard working. Their resistance to change can be a sore point in their relationship with others. They would rather be left alone to pursue their hobbies than deal with pressing personal and social problems.

Their speech is slow, deliberate, and thoughtful, and while everyone else has moved on to other topics, they are still pondering the previous idea.

The men generally find an outlet through mathematics, mechanics, accounting, and the various trades. The women often end up in dead-end jobs pushing paper around generally being frustrated in life. They can both become bogged down in the small things for lack of vision, incentive, and drive. As it has been said, "they cannot see the forest for the trees."

They are inventive if they are left alone but become discontent if pushed or if they must work by deadlines.

Their homes are a place of solace and comfort where they can putter around pursuing their personal interests in their gardens and kitchens.

When these people are unbalanced, the tension in their lives will affect them through stomach and intestinal disorders. Constipation is the main problem area as well a weakness in the heart, lungs, and bronchial organs.

7-7-5

Donald Jason Morgan Amelia Olivia Robina Alyson Ashton Joelle Madeleine Sonja Sophia Carlos Marco Brandon Renata

This is an adventuresome, quiet, deep, and intense influence. These people will quickly respond to any form of repression or injustice. Theirs is a life of profound creativity or extreme frustration with their outward circumstances. They seek to escape from a life of conformity and mediocrity. This is a restless influence that is bound to a search for excitement or for a greater meaning to life without necessarily satisfying either.

On the one hand, they desire peace of mind and a life away from the encroaching mass, while being driven by an insatiable urge for action, answers, and new experiences. Further fields always look greener and more inviting to their restless spirit. There is little potential for stability and success in this quality, in the normal sense.

They must develop their creative side or suffer the inner turmoil that results from not fitting into the mold. If there has been sufficient discipline in their lives, they could almost accomplish the impossible, otherwise the dynamic urge will be channeled along avenues of travel, excitement, and sometimes rather questionable pursuits.

They fear nothing when awakened to a challenge. The drive to succeed is powerful when properly directed but destructive if their anger is aroused. When their strong sense of justice has been violated, they will fight because they will not be put down. They are extremely independent souls who refuse to do another's bidding.

Their independence and solitary way make it difficult for them in marriage. Bouts of antisocial behavior and moods of depression are not uncommon. Going off into the woods, hiking, and exploring is the way they can regain their composure and their energy. They can excel in sports or anything that provides a challenge.

Their minds are deep and quick but overly reactive. They may not have a great deal to say, but what they do express is to the point. There is no mincing of words. They can be critical and outspoken at the drop of a hat.

They are so sensitive and finely tuned to truth and justice that any form of suppression will cause them to react. This negative influence is difficult for them to control. They are their own worst enemy when they are depressed and can be very hard on themselves as well as others when this occurs.

Through the bitterness of their personal experiences, they are driven to ask the question "Why?"

They could travel the expanse of the earth looking for answers to their questions and still never find peace of mind because of their low threshold for boredom. Their need for new experiences and new challenges undermines their capacity for stability and the time required to fully digest their studies along any particular avenue of thought.

They are susceptible to stomach problems as well as suffering in the heart, lung and bronchial area. Moods of depression can be their undoing.

7-8-6

Howard Malcolm Lorna Florence Loreen Elana Mallory Geoffrey Landon Stavros Mohan Eliana

Here we have a quality that produces a quiet, refined, and intellectual nature. Sensitivity and a deep appreciation for nature are the main attributes of these people. Their environment must be tranquil and conducive to study and reflection.

Because of their depth they are naturally philosophical. Their feelings run deep and their enquiries turn toward theories pertaining to life and religious or philosophical speculations.

They would do better to cultivate the art of writing as their verbal capacities are sometimes limited. Due to their early experiences of being misunderstood, they soon learn to keep their counsel. This eventually affects them in the natural flow of their verbal expression. Especially in their youth, their sensitivity is a matter of embarrassment when they become the focus of attention. And so it becomes preferable to say nothing rather than to experience self-consciousness.

This is a very perceptive quality. These people have a good mind and are capable of great achievement. They are serious and responsible types. Their sense of self-confidence is brought out more when they are left alone. They are not happy working in close proximity to others. When they are their own boss, they can rise to the occasion and meet the challenges that hinder success.

Their strong sense of responsibility makes them conscientious and reliable workers. They do have a tendency to take things a little too seriously at times and can be prone to worry.

Their responsible natures, combined with a natural maternal or paternal instinct, make them excellent mothers and fathers with a good sense of discipline and authority. If there is balance in the rest of their make-up, then their need for authority and responsibility easily allows them to gravitate to positions of leadership. They may not always have a great deal to say, but they do know what is going on. If there is too much imbalance, then they could become reclusive and uncommunicative.

Because they are so sensitively aware of beauty and perfection, they are easily affected by noise and the confusion of the more problematic types. The busy market place is no place for them.

In association with others they have no time for small talk. Their interest in life itself could draw them out in conversation.

Their sense of perfection can make them intolerant of others' imperfections.

They need to cultivate their innate talent for

writing their thoughts and ideas to discover the depth of their own minds and the profound creativity that lies within themselves. If they do not have a chance to develop this depth through expression, they become dreamers who follow the mystical fantasies that draw them into illusion and a feeling of spirituality—but in reality, they go nowhere. If they do not find others who understand them, they tend to become a little too reclusive. It is through creative accomplishment that they are fulfilled.

Any imbalance in their make-up would lead to excessive worry or problems affecting them through the lungs, heart, or bronchial organs.

7-9-7

Crawford Olaf Flora Doreen Norma Naomi Victoria Ramon Mona Alexa Alison Anthony Andrea Francesca Jolene Carson Dorian Carolyn Nathalie Michaela Angelica

Here we have people that are supersensitive and responsive to all forms of natural beauty but also impressionable to all forms of discord, noise, and inharmonious environments. They find it difficult to understand their own sensitivity and how to control this quality in its extreme. Their feelings are deeply touched through music, art, and all things in nature. They are romantics who respond to the moon rising or the sun setting with a sense of the mystery behind it all.

Their greatest problem lies in indulging in this sense of emotional depth, romance, mysticism, and in their imagination. If and when this occurs, they lose themselves in the realms of unreality, being pulled into a dream world where truth and fact are replaced with fantasy and make-believe. They are avid readers who find being alone with their books a replacement for friends who could never understand their deep feelings.

In a higher sense, they could be drawn to philosophy and religion with a deep appreciation for life and its meaning. They are theorists who need to understand their sensitivity as a device for divining philosophical truths.

They are naturally intuitive and capable of insights of a profound nature but only if they develop mentally. If there is no mental development, they become subject to an over-sensitive response to life by escaping into this world of idealism where nobody could live up to their expectations. At this point they become judgmental, critical, and moody. It is their moods that are their undoing. They can shut others out with an icy silence that is worse that an outburst of anger.

Being the focus of attention makes them shy and uncommunicative where their power of speech vanishes completely. This quality is the most misunderstood of all, mainly because they cannot understand themselves enough to express in words just how they feel and think, and thereafter avoid serious and meaningful contact with others. They are forced to seek within for the happiness that continually eludes them in their association with others. This could cause them to become antisocial or even reclusive.

Because of their over-sensitivity they have an interesting peculiarity. Either they are as quiet as church mice or they chatter in order to avoid revealing their feelings. On one hand they absolutely crave the quiet of their own environment where they do not have to deal with people, on the other hand they find intervals of silence in conversations so disturbing that they fill it full of nonsense and meaningless chatter. This behavior occurs unconsciously and may become a habit that they cannot control.

If there is some degree of balance in their overall make-up, they can be deep and thoughtful with a great potential for writing and creativity. When their intellect is developed, they have a perception of things and people that is most profound because they can understand and control that which pervades the quiet places.

They are vulnerable to heart, lungs, and bronchial problems such as asthma, heart attacks, and deep chest colds etc.

8-1-9

Sue Cooper Culver Karolina Johanna Jordana Rosaria Yolanda

There are two influences in these names that combine to create a vision of life that is big and broad. These people desire to do big things in life. They may not accomplish that which they desire because that depends upon their overall make-up and its balance or lack of it.

This quality lends itself to confidence and idealism and a sense of their own importance, which may be slightly inflated. The scale upon which they plan their life and vision is difficult to measure up to. They are ambitious and motivated by humanitarian principles. Their conversation and the impression they desire to portray is often inconsistent with the actual reality of their life.

First of all, from the practical and materialistic element in their character, they have a basic urge to build or create things on a grand scale. They want the best for themselves and others. The other side of their nature is compassionate and dreams of better times and a better and more just society. Unless they are empowered by a passion and a spiritual drive, this influence is difficult to live up to. Instead, it usually expresses as a personal ambition to acquire and accumulate for no other reason than to establish itself in a position of status and power.

These are noble qualities for anyone to possess. These types are intelligent, with a good insight into the minds of others. They carry themselves with poise and confidence. They can be generous, kind, and helpful, but not foolishly so. The beggar or panhandler on the street must justify his condition before these people will part with their money. They would rather contribute to the alleviation of human suffering through helping in some organized effort.

Their organizational skills should be put to use in some meaningful enterprise. They cannot be truly happy unless their work is aligned with humanitarian ideals. Their desire is to run their own show or to be in charge where no one can usurp their power. For this they must learn the right of leadership by virtue of acquiring a benevolence, motivated by a true spiritual drive.

In most cases, these people merely translate the inner urge for the common good of all as a need for personal wealth—and their compassion and love for people, as a passion for the opposite sex. It would be unkind to say they did not have good intentions, but the state of the mass mind does not encourage nobility of thought, let alone recognize it. Without a deep understanding of the meaning of life, these people, like most others, would fail to respond to the true meaning of their lives. In consequence, their visions are mostly dreams, and their wealth is usually something they talk about as an ambition. As a rule, they are pleasant and friendly with quite a positive attitude and a good heart. They have the potential for greatness if their education and their background provide the ingredients of discipline and direction.

If the rest of their names produce too much imbalance, they can become indulgent in sex and the good life and tend to be somewhat ostentatious and superior in their attitude.

Their physical weakness lies in their nervous system. For the women there could be problems in the reproductive organs.

8-2-1

Joanna Carolina Susie Montgomery Johnathan Rosanna Quentin

These names produce a personality of strength, confidence, ambition, and a tenacious ability to persevere. This is a quality that is materialistic and insensitive to the feelings of others. Their drive is directed toward personal accomplishment and they could be heard saying "Get out of my way, I'm coming through." This attitude is, of course, good for achieving their goals in a materialistic sense but not so good in securing lasting friendships. Diplomacy is not inherent in these names.

It is their capacity as "self-starters" that moves them forward so quickly in life. They do not sit around talking about what they would like to do, their pioneering urge gets them quickly started on a project. While others may take courses and do other preparatory studies before embarking on a new project, these people jump into a project and work out the problems as they arise. They can work hard and have the endurance and stamina to see a task through to its end.

The influence here is rather masculine and for a woman it could be a little hard, covering up the natural feminine aspects of her character. While being hard-nosed and competitive has a negative effect on the male persona, it can be even more devastating on the female.

This is not a sentimental or idealistic quality and will get right to the point in conversation. They know what they want to say and can be quite forthright in saying it—no beating around the bush. Their interests and their conversation revolve around their careers and their materialistic pursuits.

In love there is little romance. If their partner in marriage or business is at all idealistic, there is going to be conflict. These types are practical and quite logical. They see a spade as a spade and nothing else. Helping others with their problems is of no interest to them. Getting on with the job is the only thing that matters. Action is the keynote, not sitting around talking endlessly. To the more sensitive types this approach can be difficult to take and to deal with. Their candid manner can offend because it usually comes across with a force that sounds like a command. Being so self-confident and sure of themselves, they must be careful not to become domineering.

They naturally gravitate towards business and finance with an interest in politics. If the rest of their make-up does nothing to soften their character, then their success will be limited to the physical and material plane. Home and family can suffer with these people because they tend to lack the sensitivity and interest in dealing with social and personal issues.

Again, it should be said that all things lie in the balance. If there is not overall balance, they may become frustrated to the degree that even material success becomes impossible. Then the force of this quality will manifest as an aggressive, self-centered urge that can be quite manipulative.

Any tension in their lives will be reflected in problems affecting the senses of the head and the generative organs.

8-3-2

Lucille Hubert Elwood Fuller
Jonathan Antonia Uriel

These names provide charm, eloquence, and a desire for success without all the components necessary to bring it about. It is through people that they can get ahead, not on their own initiative. Their ambition moves them through social circles, ever striving to make the right contacts. They are open and friendly and masters of diplomacy. Lacking true self-confidence and an independent approach, they tend to believe it is their own effort that is moving them forward when in reality the credit should be given to someone else. They desire to be at the top, but without the necessary qualifications they often find themselves falling just short of their dreams. To a large extent they are followers with an ambition for leadership that can rarely be fully realized.

Their main strength is their spontaneous verbal expression and their insight into the minds and hearts of people. With a natural intuitive sense, they are helpful and capable of advising others. Being gifted with the gab, there could be a tendency to go on and on, long after the point has been made. Silence in conversation makes them uneasy and loosens their tongue to say anything in order to fill the gap. They are not too deep or philosophical in a profound sense.

Getting ahead in life is quite important to them, and having a respected social standing forms the basis for their ambition. They have a fine appreciation for material values and will strive for a high standard of living. There could be a tendency to be a little ostentatious.

When they are at work they know just the right thing to say under all circumstances. Drawing others out and making them feel relaxed comes naturally to them. Avoiding conflicts and confrontations is a matter of using their quick minds and fluid speech. They must be careful of bending the truth as a way of escaping from issues that to them are difficult and embarrassing.

Manual labor is not in the realm of their ambition. Hard work is something to be avoided. An eye for investments is always seen as security and a possible way of avoiding hard work.

People can be a great source of pleasure for them as well as a form of indulgence through idle chatter. Procrastination is their biggest challenge.

Their interests lie in areas where they can assume responsibilities and where they can express a level of authority and influence. They wish they could be leaders but may fail to gain the necessary respect they think they deserve. It is usually through organizations or institutions that they find their work, in a supportive capacity. Taking the initiative and pushing forward is what these people lack.

If other elements in their make-up drive them in their attempt to succeed, their impressionable natures can draw them into some unfortunate circumstances where they can be used or even taken advantage of in questionable dealings.

Their love of a social climate with lots of people make them vulnerable to indulgence in good foods and fine wines, etc. Any tension will affect them through kidney ailments.

8-4-3

Julie Romeo Brooke Fulbert Gunther Roberto Roscoe Rohana Rosalee

These names give strength, ambition, and an outspoken manner. Nothing holds these people back from achieving success, unless the rest of their names are unbalanced. They are confident and unafraid of pushing themselves forward. Speaking their minds comes easily, and there is power in their manner of speaking. The spoken word can either be their asset or their liability. They will not be put down by others. Their intelligence perceives the fairness or injustice of a situation and they will speak out with regards to the truth. They have a friendly and happy mental disposition and can be quite helpful to others.

Their social and loving manner requires an outlet where they can be in front of people, leading, performing, and inspiring them. They could be excellent public speakers as their strength can be quite commanding. Certainly one of the greatest human attributes anyone can possess is the power to influence—and these people have that potential. Their character contains positivity, leadership, and a certain charisma which should be used to motivate others.

If there is imbalance in their overall make-up, then

this quality can become overbearing or bossy. In that case, they can become complaining and intolerant. This usually only happens if they have not achieved a position of leadership or personal autonomy in their careers or work life. If they find themselves in subordinate roles, their unhappiness can make them intolerable.

Normally this is quite a balanced and capable influence, better for a man than a woman. For a woman, it can in some cases make her quite hard and overly independent.

Their talents are many but are best expressed where there are people and they can be in the forefront. They are good organizers and can easily take the lead. They are not timid in any way and can meet and mix with anyone.

Their appraisal of others make them good judges of character. This is not a particularly compassionate influence and at times they could find others of lesser distinction beneath them. Holding their own in debate is a product of their natural mental objectivity. Only under pressure will they speak out with a force that can be quite daunting and intimidating to the more sensitive types.

This influence combines a wealth complex with an appreciation of music, art, and color harmony. It is a nice balance. There is the danger of giving in to indulgence because of their rich taste in food and high living.

They carry themselves with poise and dignity and at the same time are not without humor. Love is a strong factor in their lives. They do not come on as being emotional types, but none the less they are drawn quite strongly to the opposite sex. Male or female, they will not take second fiddle to anyone. For this reason, the woman may wonder why she cannot keep a man in her life or she chooses to remain single.

These people could do well to cultivate a deeper appreciation of the more philosophical aspects of life, otherwise it is quite a nice quality. Any indulgence could result in problems affecting them in the generative area of their bodies or the liver.

8-5-4

Bruce Luke Buster Rosemarie Aaron Fergus Jude Georgio Miguel Annamarie Isadora

Practical and hard-nosed with a strong material-istic bent are the main characteristics of these people. They possess an ambition and a capacity for hard work. The peculiarity of this influence is that they wish they could be respected as the authority figure, delegating responsibility to others, but instead they find themselves doing all the hard work. They have a good head for detail and mathematical preci-sion. This is a quality that sees life in very practical terms and lacks a sensitivity to the artistic, musical, and philosophical side of life.

They could putter away with their hobbies and per-sonal interests to the exclusion of all around them. Their concentration and mental focus can become all-absorbing. They can really only enjoy the company of others when the discussion revolves around things that are technical, political, or things dealing with subjects pertaining to non-fiction material.

If their birth time makes them innately inspira-tional, then they would suffer from the contradiction in qualities and conflicting urges. In this unbalanced state their tendency would make them overly fussy and a bit overbearing and demanding.

Their patience makes them thorough and reliable workers, capable of finishing the things they start. They can persevere in their work, but they do not like to be pushed or forced to work on deadlines. Their methodical approach to their tasks requires time and thought in order to do the job well.

While they are bound to the grindstone, their ambitious natures are constantly visualizing bigger and better things, but alas, their lot is hard work. They could make slow and steady progress in their efforts but all the while their feelings would be of discontent.

Their ability to fix things around the house and around the office is their strong point, while fixing things in their relationship with people is not so easy. This is not a very malleable or adaptable influence. Their fixed views make it difficult to merge with others. Skepticism of anything that reaches beyond the realm of the five senses can lead these people to hide behind their hobbies and self-interests.

This is a very strong physical force that is sometimes unaware of the sensitivity that is required in dealing with the more sensitive types. On the other hand, this sometimes stubborn quality can drive them with the force of their conviction to overcome obstacles that the faint of heart would find intolerable. Their strength is often reflected in their desire for heavy solid foods which can lead to problems of overweight.

Their logical minds make them ingenious when dealing with practical and scientific matters, but they are confounded when this same logic has to be applied to religious or philosophical theory. In other words, this quality is a little too one-sided in their approach to life.

Their weakness lies in the stomach and intestinal tract with problems of constipation and allied problems.

8-6-5

June Lucie Duke Hunter Mohammad

A mbition is the key word in describing these people. They want the best and the most out of life. This relates primarily to the physical and material aspects of life. A career is uppermost in their minds. A wealth complex is a natural part of these names.

This is a self-confident and positive quality; nothing could stop them from achieving their goals. They are driven to succeed and will accomplish their aims, but they will unwittingly sacrifice their peace of mind. They cannot rest. The intensity of their drive will eventually force them into distraction. The consequence of this behavior is a disappointment in their relationships. Stability in home and family affairs will often suffer. Their personal ambitions tend to be out of balance with their sense of responsibility to others.

This is particularly hard on a woman as it tends to destroy a natural feminine influence. They can be very intimidating to the more sensitive types. Both the male and the female are quite competitive and have no trouble in confronting issues, but they do lack the sensitivity required to deal with all sides of an issue. These people tend to measure others from a predominantly material point of view.

Giving orders is preferable to taking orders with these people. They would not stay in a subordinate role for very long. Their ambition would drive them into positions where they are free to promote and experience the freedom that comes with being their own boss. Sales, travel, and the promotion of their own ideas is always behind their efforts to achieve financial independence.

Money is the strong motivating force behind their ambitious nature. Like most people, their fear or overconcern with daily responsibilities overshadows a deeper truth that is best described in the Christian saying, "We should seek first the Kingdom of Heaven which lies within" if we are ever to realize a peace that could indeed pass understanding.

In the highest sense, they have the responsibility to use their natural leadership potential and their material pursuits for the betterment of life and for the greater good for all. Invariably their focus is centered on personal accumulation. Imbalance must always produce its just consequence.

Unfortunately they are driven. And in the process, they may become unbalanced. Trying to relax at times becomes impossible and will eventually take its toll on their health.

Their minds are quick and astute when it comes to figures, finance, and logic. They have a strong sense of justice and fair play. If the rest of their make-up provided some idealism, their courage and drive could produce tremendous good in life; otherwise they merely spend their energies on a purely personal level.

This restless intensity can eventually wear them out. Then they can become overbearing and controlling, finding relationships difficult to deal with. They are extremely independent and refuse to conform to traditional values that might undermine their sense of individuality.

Their stomach and generative organs are their weak points.

8-7-6

Muriel Huntley Ruben
Humphrey Montana

L eadership and organization are the main qualities of these names. These people are strong,
confident, and self-sufficient. They have no intention
of taking a back seat to anyone. If there is balance in
the rest of their make-up, their ambition will take
them a long way in reaching their goals. If there is
imbalance and they are forced into positions of sub-
ordination, they will fight and the strength of their
names will manifest as bossiness or as a domineering
quality.

As they climb their ladder towards success they
have no fear of taking the initiative and assuming
responsibilities without being told. The power of
their character can be intimidating to the more sensitive types. They understand people and are good at
delegating responsibilities. The main drive in their
lives is to get ahead, work hard, and become financially independent. There is no time for foolishness.
Their lives are centered around their careers and
their material ambitions.

They are good at figures and balancing the books.
Everything must be accounted for, nothing should be
out of place. As bosses or as parents they are hard task

masters, but not unkind.

They have a strong desire to help and to teach others. The urge to instruct others is primary to their success and their happiness and must be cultivated and brought out. Their strong sense of authority must be respected. They work successfully only if they have complete control of their responsibilities.

If they have not worked themselves into a position of being the boss, they will naturally be unhappy and make everyone else miserable because of their negative tendency to interfere and push people around in order to get their way. Again, this is only if there is a degree of imbalance in the rest of their names.

Very few people can do things as efficiently as these types. They know it and therefore it is hard for others to live up to their expectations. This name influence can be a little strong for a female and tend to destroy her natural feminine qualities. She could be quite overbearing.

These people can be active in community work or volunteers when anything needs to be done. They are intelligent and quick to take control where it is required. Their natural maternal or paternal quality makes them good mothers and fathers, and their strong sense of justice and fair play will make them formidable opponents when fighting for a cause.

They are leaders and must use their natural gifts for the benefit of others and not become lost in the pursuit of wealth and materiality purely for selfish interests. Their practical natures should be balanced with idealism and a higher motive. They are good judges of people, and it is this ability that lies at the basis of their spirituality. Mental objectivity and the power to see things dispassionately gives them a great responsibility. They are not easily drawn into arguments as this form of conduct is beneath them.

They possess the great power to influence others. They must use it wisely.

They are generally quite healthy. Any weakness will affect them in the generative organs.

8-8-7

Russell Eleanor Dolores Unice Dakota Harmonia

O ur first impression of these people is their quiet strength. They know how to use silence to the best advantage. Ambition, combined with their appreciation of beauty and refinement, can take these people to great levels of success. It is not necessary for these people to say in words what they want out of life because they are people of action. If they have a failing it is that they say too little and can be misunderstood by what they do say.

Personally they are refined, with expensive tastes and an appreciation for the value of money and its power to get them what they want. They love the earth and all its bounty including the beauty of sunsets and the rising moon and what it suggests.

They have confidence and quickly rise to become their own bosses because of their efficiency and their natural business acumen. Working with others is not easy for them as they are independent and quite capable of working for themselves and figuring things out without interference from others.

Their self-sufficiency could become a liability when they realize they do things better than others; thus, they end up doing things themselves. They do have the ability to organize others but are not naturally social creatures.

It is difficult to feel easy and relaxed in their environment because they say very little unless it is in regard to things philosophical or of a deeper nature concerning their personal interests. It is almost as if at times they look down at others. The truth is they are intelligent and perceptive and do not concern themselves with small talk or gossip. At such times they become disinterested, somewhat aloof and detached from their surroundings.

Their love of nature and the earth make them superb gardeners.

Walks in the woods have a way of rejuvenating them. Flowers, art, and music can touch them deeply. Their work should involve something with nature. They have the ability to capitalize on their personal interests and turn them into money. If they cannot work for the love of work, they cannot succeed nor could they endure mediocrity.

They have concentration and discipline, which helps them achieve almost anything they desire. Writing could be an excellent way for them to express their deeper feelings and thoughts.

In relationships, they can have difficulty communicating. Even though they know so much, expressing it verbally is quite difficult. It isn't long before they find themselves responding to others' faults with a silence that can be very disturbing.

Unconsciously they can become judgmental, and ultimately this leads to an eroding relationship. If this happens too often they can turn away from relationships and become somewhat reclusive, choosing to remain a single person. If their birth time indicates a naturally social nature, they will suffer the consequence of the imbalance.

Any weakness will affect them in the heart, lungs, and bronchial organs as well as the generative and female organs.

8-9-8

Julien Rupert Lucile Ramona Monroe Alexandra Justine Madonna Dudley

These people combine a strong masculine influence with a commanding presence. They are full of self-confidence and a sense of their own power. Working for other people is beneath them. They are ambitious and capable of getting what they want. Being so bold, they must be careful not to step on people in order to get their own way. Their personal ambition can blind them to the comforts of home and hearth. Family and marital interests usually take second place to their insatiable drive for success and financial independence.

They stand above others in leadership and in their abilities to organize people. They must wonder at their sense of superiority as they look down at us mere mortals. Looking down their noses could be a problem. Using their innate potential for helping others less fortunate is not always a consideration as they climb their ladder of success.

This is a dispassionate quality with the power to see clearly into the minds of others and a tendency to judge from their lofty positions of power or assumed superiority. In the highest sense, they make good judges because they are not influenced by emotional displays. This allows them a level of mental objectivity and sound reasoning. In marriage, their more emotional spouses will be starved for affection. At the same time these people are problem-solvers and quick to understand underlying motives because of their mental insight. Unfortunately, their problem solving applies mostly to their careers. If there are problems in marriage, they tend to escape into their work.

They do not shirk from work. Their careers are their main focus, particularly if they are the boss. This is their life. If there is an imbalance that finds them in a subordinate role in life, they can become quite fierce and domineering. Home and family are not priorities unless a maternal or paternal urge is a part of some other aspect of their make-up. This being the first name, it is the compelling force. Once they begin to make money and experience the power of it, there is no end to their need to acquire more.

They have a desire for the best that money can buy and have an eye for a bargain. They can spend lavishly on nice things, while at the same time, they are frugal and will account for every penny spent. In looking others over, there can be a tendency to measure them from a material standard. In other words, you are not getting ahead in life if you do not have money. This negative aspect depends upon the degree of balance of the whole character.

Bringing people together is easy and enjoyable for

them. They can delegate responsibilities, hire, and fire others without a moment of embarrassment. They have the power to influence people for the good or otherwise.

Being a strong masculine quality, the female tends to suffer in relationships. She will take a back seat to no man. In this day and age this may seem admirable, but when the woman competes with the male force, all are bound to lose.

Through tension these people will suffer through the generative organs and experience problems in conception and reproduction.

9-1-1

Nick Claude Irwin Iris Cindy Phillip Kristin Anatolia Jiri Jaques Dmitri Gil

Deep within these people lies a profound and a powerful emotion. Love is at the root of their feelings. This emotional force will either express as a physical force through the sexual channel, or if they can develop mentally, they can raise it to a higher level. They are profoundly motivated by a humanitarian urge.

Compassion as well as passion is a driving force in their lives. Their constant thought is to be able to do something useful for the benefit of others and not just waste their lives doing menial tasks. They are self-starters with a great capacity for work.

Suffering humanity touches their heartstrings and compels them to reach out to serve the needs of those unfortunates. Their own need to experience affection and love is quite strong and could become misplaced if they do not develop mentally. Their lessons are difficult because the channeling of this emotional force upward toward love—as a universal force for the purpose of serving humanity—is often experienced as a powerful need for personal love.

When this occurs they become absorbed or preoccupied with romantic delusions. No one could ever satisfy their idealistic notions of love. When they do fall in love, few could ever equal their spontaneous urge to give and express the little things that mean so much. These feelings are usually short-lived.

These people exhibit a duality that is most difficult to combine. First of all, they draw from this deeply emotional nature that needs to express itself to all of humanity through love and compassion. Unfortunately, the other side of their personality tends to make them very independent and concerned about freeing themselves from commitments to anything or anyone. They could, consequently, find working with people frustrating and difficult.

With all of this emotion to contend with, they can find their verbal expression blocked. Sometimes there is just nothing to say for fear of it coming out garbled, or it may express with such force that they fear their own temper. This limitation in their verbal expression can be a great source of misunderstanding with others.

If they fail to succeed at combining their emotional needs and maintaining their independence, then they will suffer a great emotional repression.

They must have their independence; without it their lives can be hell. The negative side of all this emotion expresses primarily as self-pity and self-depreciation. They have the capacity for the highest expressions of universal love or the lowest expressions of sexual degradation.

At their highest, they have a deep appreciation for music and art. They also have a strong need to get away by themselves and to exert themselves through some physical challenge in order to release the pent-up emotion.

They exhibit the mental quality that governs the nervous system. If they cannot balance out their lives, they can suffer from all forms of nervous disorders as well as being affected in the senses of the head.

9-2-2

Doug Audrey Phyllis Ivy Beau Chi Kirby Raquel Guido

These names bring out a soft, passive, or feminine influence. They are all sweetness and charm. Their aim in life is to please. They couldn't hurt anyone if they wanted to because they would suffer in another's suffering. Every vibration in the atmosphere of another is registered in the emotions of these people. They are impressionable and responsive to the ways and thoughts of all people. Their response is naturally and spontaneously an effort to make or keep the peace. They are sensitive and easily hurt. It is for this reason that they become extremely accommodating, if only to avoid confrontation and the ensuing embarrassment.

In some cases where the innate quality through the time of birth produces an urge for strength and independence, then the conflict of the two opposing natures could produce extreme passivity at times or moments of aggression as a result of the frustration due to the imbalance. This represents the two natures fighting against each other in a negative expression.

They do not have much confidence or the ability to assert themselves, nor can they easily become self-motivated or initiate action.

It is for them to follow or to support others. This can be very hard on those types who are natural leaders by birth. Every aspect or facet of human consciousness is a part of the whole, but when there is an imbalance or predominance of these qualities it makes life difficult.

These people make excellent hosts and have a way with people that is both charming and disarming. They can draw others out and dispel their gloom in an instant. They can say things that are appropriate and just what one wants to hear because they are intuitive to one's every thought and feeling. We can find ourselves revealing our life histories or our most intimate thoughts to these people because they are sympathetic, open and have the ability to listen with interest, or that is what we are lead to believe. Sometimes it is just because they are so passive and they find it is better to listen than to speak out and upset anyone. In this attitude, they are often used because they cannot stand up for themselves and express their own strong feelings about things.

Keeping a confidence is not their strong point. Talking about little things can become a preoccupation. They must guard against gossip.

They are dreamers and idealists who have a vision of life that they themselves might never achieve. Love and charity and tenderness are their strong points. Procrastination and being late are the negative aspects of their character. Hard work, manual labor, or domestic responsibilities are approached with the idea "manyana."

They are affectionate and full of love for all people. Their eyes are bright and their smile is genuine and inviting. It is easy to "fall" in love with them. They must beware of being taken advantage of.

This quality is particularly weak for a man because it destroys his self-confidence. Getting his hands dirty is most disagreeable.

Their kidneys can suffer when their lack of discipline leads to indulgence in sweet foods.

9-3-3

Chris Lou Susanne Manuel Li Laurie Petula Sigrid Eugene Kristy Ricky

E motion could be described as the medium for feeling, a state of awareness before thought. Only through building a strong mind could these people ever hope to control or bring an emotional stability into their lives. They feel everything so deeply that they become impressionable to the over-powering influence of their emotions. When they are inspired, they reach great highs which they cannot sustain. Conversely, when they feel depressed, they suffer the depths of despair. Their life is a series of mood swings.

Only through music and art can they succeed in channeling this enormous emotional force and, therefore, find a modicum of stability. The motivating force in their lives is love and self-expression. This requires an outlet through inspiring and serving others.

Their need for love becomes crucial and almost impossible to satisfy. Their natural idealism and compassion is the only thing that could save them from becoming totally preoccupied with the search for personal love. It is through some humanitarian endeavor that they could successfully express this love force, otherwise it would manifest more as a physically sexual force or as an insatiable craving or longing for a personal love experience. The lesson for these people, as for all others, is to see the beauty in their lovers before, during, and long after a sexual union—or forever become misguided into believing that somewhere out there is one person who will satisfy their egos and they will bask in the glory of loving bliss forever.

These people suffer from an impracticality that could only be overcome with the strength that comes through discipline. They are fine and motivated when they are inspired but find it extremely difficult to finish the things they start. The spirit behind any endeavor makes itself known only after many years of consistent effort, and then only if the motive is correct and it is given to life freely.

Concentration and attention to detail is not a part of these people's characters. Staying with anything long enough to succeed is almost impossible. House work, yard work, and the like become pure drudgery.

Play is very important for them whether they are young or old. As performers they have the chance to experience the joy of giving. When this occurs their happiness overflows and their generosity, warmth, and kindness are expressed. As a reciprocal act of kindness, they would give the shirt off their backs. They are sensitive and easily hurt.

Being so emotional, their efforts are scattered.

They do not look after things and cannot save money to save their souls. Despite their lack of success, they are eternally optimistic. They have the ability to look to the brighter side of things and can be quite lucky at times.

The tendency to indulge in the physical appetites can lead to problems in the liver. Being party types, alcohol can lead to their downfall. Tension will also affect them through their nervous systems.

9-4-4

Kirk Clint Kitty Sybil Vi Louis Miri Brigid Quon Jacques Murdock Lily Kit

I dealism and perfection are the two words that best describe these people. Their work has to have a greater meaning to it, and then they will pursue it as specialists. Whether it is in the home, office, or in the field, they will approach their task with meticulous scrutiny. Everything must be just so, nothing out of place. Unfortunately, in these influences there is something out of place. There is an intensity of emotion that is always directed to the physical plane of facts and details. Their idealism is somewhat thwarted and forced to express through perfection in details. This quality arouses a skepticism about anything that does not relate to the practical world of fact.

They have very definite views about life which make them quite inflexible. Their conversation does not flow easily because of their fixed views. There is no give and take because they cannot, as we say, "think on their feet." They have to ponder over a thing for a long time before it becomes established as a fact in their minds. Through the hard road of experience, an idea slowly forms and takes root in their consciousness. Therefore, in conversation they cannot accept another's thought unless it comes within the range of some personal experience. Debating is not within the realm of their talents because their minds work too slowly, and they cannot give their opponent the benefit of the doubt.

Their penchant for detail could earn them the reputation for being fussy. They could do well in occupations that require a lot of research or attention to detail, as long as it was motivated by some greater purpose. If it was not, their frustrations would become intolerable.

They have a desire to work to some greater purpose but invariably find themselves working out the problems of life in some capacity that can feel like drudgery. They possess an underlying humanitarianism that can not always be fully expressed. In truth, they should be teachers in some religious or philosophical way but usually end up preoccupied by the mundane. If there is some degree of balance in the sum total of their names, they could specialize in a field with some degree of success.

The emotional quality behind this influence is quite strong in its love nature. When it cannot be expressed fully through its idealism, it will seek an avenue through the physical plane. If these people do not strive to understand their deep need for love and the implications of their strong sex drive, their nervous systems will suffer. At times this nervous energy can be very unsettling.

They are dreamers who live for a better day and

brighter future, but in the meantime they work hard knowing full well that nothing comes from nothing. Their security is measured in dollars and cents, and their frugality accounts for every penny earned. Their materialism can override their spiritual values.

This is a very logical quality that is dictated first by personal need and secondly by their idealism. They must not lose themselves in the little inconsequentials of life.

Their nervous system as well as blockages in the intestinal tract are their physical weaknesses.

9-5-5

Jim Sid Wilf King Virgil Dorothea Rick Kristi Marcellus Glynis

These names produce a quality of extremes. They could be deeply religious or be completely turned off to orthodox religious views. Whatever strikes them at the root of their emotions at any particular time, leaves a deep impression. Regardless of their orientation, they are full of compassion for human suffering and not beyond doing something about it. They are temperamental and subject to moments of great inspiration and then can drop to the depths of depression and self-pity.

This is a driving and restless force that is difficult to stabilize. Things that go wrong are felt deeply, and it is impossible to shake them off quickly. Their tempers can be aroused with the drop of a hat. They cannot take criticism, but find themselves dishing it out at the slightest provocation. Their minds are quick and sharp and quite impulsive. If their morality directs their actions, there will still be a suppression of feeling due to their intense emotional natures.

Taking risks is easy for them. They do not even consider the consequences until things occur. What they want they will go after and work things out as it develops. Their courage and their convictions allow them to accomplish a great deal, but there is usually a price that has to be paid. They learn quickly but at a cost. Their strong sense of justice can move them into action against the wrongs of life and for that their compensation is crucifixion. The intensity behind their actions is usually returned with equal force. They can be daring and committed to a cause in the face of great odds. Their anger can be their initial motivation in pursuing that cause, but they must realize that the truth will never be found in the battle if their anger remains. In this case their anger becomes their downfall. Getting even or foolishly defending our egos will absolutely blind us to the truth of any situations.

These types are idealistic and their work must have a higher reason to it, otherwise they are easily bored and then they become restless. Their quick minds and their compassion need an outlet through some humanitarian endeavor.

They have a strong need to experience love and have a great capacity for love. If they do not have a solid grounding in the way of life and love, this force can run away with them. There is a potential tendency for fanaticism here. Once the doors to love or religion are opened through some experience, their feeling can take them to extremes. They can become inspired and take their needs and their beliefs to a point beyond reality or balance. If they lack a strong moral principle, then sex can become an obsession.

When they are inspired there is nothing they couldn't do. They are clever and insightful, but when they are down, their self-pity can move them to the depths of despair.

They are always on the move. Their restless minds are continually drawing them into new experiences. The lack of balance through emotional instability forever moves them to search for peace of mind which may elude them. Their nervous system suffers the consequences of this imbalance.

9-6-6

Kim Pauline Claudine Billy Tim Laurel Juno Jin

Here we find people who are genuine caring types with a strong maternal or paternal nature. They would give far more than their fair share in order to reconcile any differences they might have with others. Their sense of responsibility commits them to any task with a heart-felt loyalty. They are kind and generous with an open heart to all people in need. Their serious dispositions could border on excessive worry if there is too much imbalance in the rest of their make-up, otherwise this is a very nice quality.

Their deepest motivations arise from their desire to help others. They are teachers who possess compassion and a sympathetic connection to those in need. Their out-pouring of love is felt by those whom they contact and help, or for that matter we all feel their open and caring quality.

With many people love is a very selfish desire, yet with these people it is strongly imbued with caring and a sense of responsibility. Their family and friends mean everything to them. If there are losses experienced in close associations, they are devastated, and their grieving usually goes on longer than is healthy.

They must learn the higher aspects of love and not become too possessive of family and friends.

They are intelligent and aware of others' short-comings. They have a strong compulsion to correct others where they see the need. Their sense of authority and keen perspective of things make them excellent mothers, fathers, or teachers, and they are good disciplinarians. At times this desire to correct others must be checked so that it does not become an interference or hindrance, rather than a help. Being too bossy could be a problem. They care so deeply that it could turn into a situation where they do everything for everyone because they feel no one could do it as well as themselves, or habitually they are forever picking up after everyone else. Taking things too seriously could alienate others.

They have an inspirational nature that requires an outlet through music and dance, otherwise their seri-ousness can make them a little gloomy. Their warmth and love can bring the best out of people. Any work they do must be motivated by a humanitarian ideal or they will be frustrated. If their lives become a matter of domestic routine, they can become carping and critical. They must work for the benefit of all, in an environment where they are teaching, loving and administering to the needy.

Their love knows no bounds if they discover its power as a force that is awakened through selfless giving. If their love turns too much towards the emotional and physical regions, they are bound to lose those things they love the most.

They must be their own boss, in charge of the situation at all times. Nothing pleases them as much as having people come to them with questions. When their authority is not questioned, they are at their best. They must earn this respect. Their intelligence and common sense must be expressed in leadership. If their minds and intellect are developed, these people can achieve a great deal, otherwise they fall prey to their negative side which can express as intense worry and nervous exhaustion.

9-7-7

Ingrid Maurice Bruno Lilly Philip Jimmy Jill Flint Fritz Liv

These names produce a highly idealistic, sensitive, caring, and humanitarian nature. They are very finely tuned to beauty, art, and music. Their depth of feeling runs so deep that it becomes impossible to control. Their emotions lead them into extreme highs and lows. When this occurs, they suffer a depletion which causes depression and self-pity.

Because of this profound depth of emotion or feeling, they will have the most beautiful love experiences without ever knowing how to sustain them. Theirs is the lesson of universal love, but invariably they become lost in personal love that has its basis in self-gratification.

This level of sensitivity will sometimes open them up to the psychic realm. They are subject to visions and religious phenomena that can make them deeply religious in an orthodox or unorthodox way. Trying to explain to others how they feel most often leads to misunderstandings, and eventually they just do not communicate their feelings and experiences. Seldom are they taken seriously.

If they are to ever live to the higher side of this emotional sensitivity, they must cultivate their talents along musical, literary, and artistic avenues. They must close the door to the psychic planes or be drawn into the realms of mysticism where they will remain a prisoner to sensations, speculations, theories, and illusions that have no basis in reality. At times though, they can be left with a profound insight due to the depth of their experience. Their lives lie in the balance between emotion and reason, between illusion and reality.

Because of a limitation in verbal expression, they can find an outlet for their feelings through acting and drama. Their deep empathy or sympathy with their characters can be portrayed very convincingly and leave a strong impression with their audience.

They are so sympathetic to the problems of others that there is always the danger of picking up the problems of those who they are in sympathy with. Their compassion for others is their motive for seeking work along humanitarian lines. If they had to survive in the market place with its noise and confusion for too long, it would drive them crazy.

They love and long for the tranquillity of nature with its animals and its natural beauties. Theirs is not an easy life in this world of materiality and confusion.

They consider their great depth of sensitivity as an asset, but it really becomes their greatest liability because it is the source of all their problems. Their moods, depressions, and illnesses are all related to their inability to control this highly emotional nature.

Love is the motivating force in their lives. They have an enormous capacity to give, but when it does not work out they can fall to pieces and grieve longer than is healthy. The negative element here is possessiveness and jealousy.

The imbalance can lead to problems affecting the heart, lungs, and bronchial organs, as well as nervous disorders.

9-8-8

Bill Samuel Austen Lauren Wing Lin

"**B**ig" is the word that best describes these people. They talk big, dream big, and unconsciously give others an impression of themselves that is often larger than life. Their heart is big, but they must be aware that their generosity is not motivated by an impulse to impress. It is their extreme idealism, combined with their material and political interests, that causes them to exaggerate their own importance.

Their desire to serve life in some way is quite sincere. Their business and personal interests are always imbued with the thought of service. They are aware and interested in the events of the community politically and socially, and desire to be involved. As organizers, they can be quite magnanimous. While they have a wealth complex and desire to be financially independent, the balance of the whole name determines their degree of success.

This influence is not deep or intellectual. Their idealism tends to govern their thoughts more on a level of theory than on a level of practical reality. This is not to say that their business dealings are not practical. They have an astute and shrewd mind for making money, but even then they must be cautious of letting their idealism carry them into unsound propositions.

If there is too much imbalance, then their talk belies their intentions. They will attempt to give the impression of knowing far more than they actually do. They have a confidence and a bravado that isn't always followed through with action.

As leaders they are good-natured and helpful. They love their family and friends and are good providers. At times their generosity can exceed their pocketbook, while at other times they can be quite stingy with their money, accounting for every penny.

They enjoy the good things of life, the creature comforts as they say. They are not past putting on a little show with their wealth and their possessions. It could be said that they have a charitable nature, but it may not come from the depths of some profound compassion. They tend to be materialists first and their religious convictions and affiliations take second place. It is to organizations or charities that they are at times compelled to give, not from a person-to-person situation, unless it is in the family.

For the most part, these people are quite pleasant, helpful, and good-hearted, but it is the combination of influences in these names that prevent a real depth of mind. Even in love they cannot easily plumb the depths of another's soul to arouse an appropriate response. They may desire to go deeply into a romance with the opposite sex, however mental or

spiritual intimacy is difficult for them. In consequence, their lack of romance is replaced by a need
for sexual completion, which expresses primarily
through the physical body.

These people have poise, confidence, and a
worldly outlook on life. Their main interests lie in the
field of business and politics. They are forever
dreaming of a better way of life. They are mostly arm-
chair politicians who firmly believe their political idealism could change the world. They love good food
and drink, and indulgence could be a weakness.

9-9-9

Dick Phil Cliff Mick Duane Nikki Jacquelyn Nils Min Kip

L ove is the prime motivation of these people. They are high-strung, emotional, generous, and at times very giving. Compassion and an automatic response to the suffering masses is at the basis of their life and their love. Being so very emotional, they find it difficult to maintain stability and an even keel in their affairs.

When these people fall in love they experience the very highest and will literally give the shirt off their backs to show their gratitude. Their kindness and generosity know no bounds as long as the love lasts.

No one experiences such despair and grief for the loss of love through death, estrangement, or separation. Their grieving can go on long past the point of reason. Their emotions can take them to the very highest as well as sink them into the depths of despair, where self-pity can obsess them.

This influence governs the nervous system and often puts them in a state of nervous agitation or a feeling of being unsettled, sometimes without knowing why.

The lesson they must learn is a very difficult one. It is that of channeling this emotional force of love and raising it to a universal level. If they do not, then it reverts to an insatiable need for personal love, wherein the sexual element can become a preoccupation.

The key to their success is in their humanitarianism. When they learn to give unselfishly and ask for nothing in return, they will then begin to understand the enormous power in living for others. There is nothing they would not do to help or administer to someone in need. They feel the helplessness of the sufferer and are compelled through compassion and love to respond. To experience the suffering of the smallest creatures brings tears to their eyes.

They are easy marks for a handout to all kinds of panhandlers and shysters looking for an easy buck. Finding the difference between sympathy and compassion is not easy for them.

Inspiration is their incentive and their motivation in life. Music and drama touch them deeply. Their lesson is to raise their emotional natures through drama, art, and music in an effort to inspire others.

They are drawn toward religious or philosophical studies and can occasionally have some profound moments of insight. Because of their extremes, fanaticism in their pursuits must be watched. Like most people who tend toward emotionalism, these people must guard against living exclusively in their feelings and their imagination.

Invariably, they are called upon to give, give, and

give some more. In the highest sense, they are spiritual teachers with the potential to move others through their charisma and their compassion. Unfortunately, what usually occurs to bring them down is the natural swing of their over-emotional natures. There is so much intensity that it can cause a level of instability and destroy their best efforts.

As has been said, this quality affects the entire nervous system and can produce all forms of nervous disorders.

NAME DIRECTORY

IF YOUR NAME IS NOT IN THE FOLLOWING LIST OF NAMES, REFER TO THE SECTION "WORKING OUT YOUR NAME" ON PAGE 22 AND DETERMINE THE THREE-NUMBER FORMULA OF YOUR NAME THAT CORRESPONDS TO THE THREE NUMBERS AT THE TOP OF EACH ANALYSIS.

Aaron 8-5-4	Alexis 6-1-7
Abdul 4-9-4	Alf 1-9-1
Adam 2-8-1	Alfonso 4-6-1
Adrian 2-9-2	Alfred 6-4-1
Adriana 3-9-3	Ali 1-3-4
Adriene 2-9-2	Alice 6-6-3
Adrienne2-5-7	Alicia 2-6-8
Agnes 6-4-1	Alisa 2-4-6
Ahmad 2-7-9	Alison 7-9-7
Al 1-3-4	Allan 2-2-4
Alan 2-8-1	Allen 6-2-8
Alanna 3-4-7	Allison 7-3-1
Alastair 3-6-9	Alma 2-7-9
Albert 6-7-4	Alvin 1-3-4
Alec 6-6-3	Alyse 6-2-8
Alex 6-9-6	Alyson 7-7-5
Alexa 7-9-7	Amanda 3-4-7
Alexander 3-9-3	Amber 6-6-3
Alexandra 8-9-8	Ambrose 3-7-1

Amelia 7-7-5

Amy 1-2-3

Anastasia 4-9-4

Anatolia 9-1-1

Andre 6-9-6

Andrea 7-9-7

Andrew 6-5-2

Andy 1-7-8

Angel 6-6-3

Angela 7-6-4

Angelica 7-9-7

Angelina 7-2-9

Angelo 3-6-9

Angus 4-4-8

Anita 2-7-9

Ann 1-1-2

Anna 2-1-3

Annamaria 4-5-9

Annamarie 8-5-4

Anne 6-1-7

Annette 2-5-7

Anthony 7-9-7

Anton 7-3-1

Antonia 8-3-2

Antonio 4-3-7

Antony 7-1-8

Anu 4-5-9

April 1-1-2

Arael 7-3-1

Aretha 7-1-8

Arlene 2-8-1

Arnold 7-3-1

Aron 7-5-3

Arran 2-5-7

Arthur 4-1-5

Aruna 5-5-1

Ashleigh 6-9-6

Ashley 6-1-7

Ashton 7-7-5

Asmena 7-1-8

Aubrey 9-9-9

Audrey 9-2-2

Austen 9-8-8

Austin 4-8-3

Avolon 4-3-7

Badru 4-6-1

Bailey 6-3-9

Barbara 3-4-7

Barry 1-9-1

Basil 1-6-7

Beatrice 2-7-9

Beau 9-2-2

Becky 5-5-1

Ben 5-7-3

Benjamin 6-8-5

Bernard 6-2-8

Bernice 1-1-2

Bert 5-4-9

Beryl 5-3-8

Bess 5-4-9

Beth 5-3-8

Bethany 6-6-3

Betsy 5-3-8

Bette 1-6-7

Bettina 6-2-8

Betty 5-4-9

Bev 5-6-2

Bevin 5-2-7

Bianca 2-1-3

Bill 9-8-8

Billie -5-84

Billy 9-6-6

Bjorn 6-8-5

Blaine 6-1-7

Blair 1-5-6

Blake 6-7-4

Bob 6-4-1

Bobbi 6-6-3

Bonnie 2-3-5

Boyd 6-4 1

Brad 1-6-7

Braden 6-2-8

Bradley 6-7-4

Brandon 7-7-5

Brayden 6-9-6

Breanna 7-3-1

Brenda 6-2-8

Brendan 6-7-4

Brennan 6-8-5

Brent 5-9-5

Brett 5-6-2

Brian 1-7-8

Bridget 5-6-2

Brigid 9-4-4

Brigitte 5-4-9

Brittany 1-9-1

Brock 6-7-4

Bronwyn 6-6-3

Brooke 8-4-3

Brooks 3-5-8

Brown 6-3-9

Bruce 8-5-4

Bruno 9-7-7

Bryan 1-5-6

Bryce 5-3-8

Brynn 7-3-1

Buck 3-7-1

Bud 3-6-9

Burgess 8-2-1

Burl 3-5-8

Burt 3-4-7

Buster 8-5-4

Byron 6-5-2

Caitlin 1-4-5

Callum 4-4-8

Calvin 1-6-7

Cameron 3-3-6

Camilla 2-4-6

Camille 6-4-1

Candace 7-6-4

Candice 6-6-3

Cara 2-3-5

Carl 1-6-7

Carla 2-6-8

Carlos 7-7-5

Carly 1-4-5

Carmela 7-1-8

Carmen 6-3-9

Carol 7-6-4

Carole 3-6-9

Carolina 8-2-1

Caroline 3-2-5

Carolyn 7-9-7

Carrie 6-3-9

Carson 7-9-7

Casey 6-2-8

Cassandra 3-5-8

Cassius 4-6-1

Catherine 2-9-2

Cathy 1-2-3

Cecil 5-9-5

Cecilia 6-9-6

Cecily 5-7-3

Celeste 6-9-6

Chandra 2-2-4

Chantal 2-3-5

Charlene 2-1-3

Charles 6-6-3

Charlie 6-5-2

Charlotte 3-9-3

Charmaine 7-2-9

Chelsea 2-6-8

Chelsey 1-4-5

Chen 5-7-3

Cheryl 5-3-8

Chi 9-2-2

Chloe 2-5-7

Chris 9-3-3

Christian 1-1-2

Christina 1-1-2

Christopher 2-2-4

Chuck 3-7-1

Cindy 9-1-1

Claire 6-6-3

Clara 2-6-8

Clarence 2-5-7

Claud 4-1-5

Claude 9-1-1

Claudia 5-1-6

Claudine 9-6-6

Clay 1-4-5

Clayton 7-2-9

Cleo 2-6-8

Cliff 9-9-9

Clifford 6-4-1
Clint 9-4-4
Clinton 6-9-6
Clive 5-1-6
Clyde 5-8-4
Cody 6-5-2
Cole 2-6-8
Colin 6-2-8
Collin 6-5-2
Connie 2-4-6
Connor 3-4-7
Conrad 7-3-1
Constance 3-1-4
Cooper 8-1-9
Cora 7-3-1
Coral 7-6-4
Corbin 6-1-7
Cordelia 3-1-4
Coretta 3-7-1
Cory 6-1-7
Courtenay 6-8-5
Craig 1-1-2
Crawford 7-9-7
Crystal 1-7-8
Culver 8-1-9
Curt 3-5-8
Curtis 3-6-9
Cynthia 1-7-8
Cyrus 3-2-5

Daisy 1-3-4
Dakota 8-8-7
Dale 6-7-4
Dalton 7-5-3
Damien 6-4-1
Damon 7-4-2
Dan 1-9-1
Dana 2-9-2
Daniela 7-3-1
Daniella 7-6-4
Danielle 2-6-8
Danny 1-3-4
Darcie 6-7-4
Darcy 1-5-6
Darius 4-5-9
Darlene 2-3-5
Darrell 6-1-7
Darren 6-9-6
Darryl 1-5-6
Dave 6-8-5
David 1-3 4
Davinder 6-8-5
Dayle 6-5-2
Dean 6-9-6
Debbie 1-8-9
Deborah 3-5-8
Deirdre 1-8-9
Del 5-7-3
Demetrius 4-2-6

Denis 5-1-6
Denise 1-1-2
Dennis 5-6-2
Derek 1-6-7
Derrick 5-9-5
Desiree 6-5-2
Devon 2-4-6
Diana 2-9-2
Diane 6-9-6
Dianne 6-5-2
Dick 9-9-9
Dillon 6-6-3
Dina 1-9-1
Dinah 1-8-9
Dione 2-9-2
Dmitri 9-1-1
Dolly 6-8-5
Dolores 8-8-7
Dominic 6-7-4
Donald 7-7-5
Donna 7-5-3
Donovan 4-9-4
Dora 7-4-2
Doreen 7-9-7
Dorian 7-9-7
Dorothea 9-5-5
Dorothia 4-5-9
Dorothy 3-3-6
Doug 9-2-2

Drew 5-9-5
Duane 9-9-9
Dudley 8-9-8
Dugald 4-9-4
Duke 8-6-5
Duncan 4-8-3
Dunstan 4-8-3
Dustin 3-3-6
Earl 6-3-9
Earle 2-3-5
Ed 5-4-9
Eddie 1-8-9
Edgar 6-2-8
Edith 5-5-1
Edmond 2-8-1
Edna 6-9-6
Edward 6-4-1
Edwin 5-5-1
Eileen 6-8-5
Elaine 2-8-1
Elana 7-8-6
Elanor 3-8-2
Eleanor 8-8-7
Eli 5-3-8
Eliana 7-8-6
Elias 6-4-1
Elijah 6-3-9
Elissa 6-5-2
Eliza 6-2-8

Elizabeth 2-5-7

Elke 1-5-6

Ellen 1-2-3

Elliot 2-8-1

Elma 6-7-4

Eloisa 3-4-7

Elsa 6-4-1

Elspeth 1-3-4

Elva 6-7-4

Elwood 8-3-2

Emily 5-5-1

Emma 6-8-5

Enid 5-9-5

Eric 5-3-8

Erica 6-3-9

Ernest 1-8-9

Errin 5-5-1

Errol 2-3-5

Ester 1-3-4

Esther 1-2-3

Ethel 1-4-5

Eugene 9-3-3

Eunice 4-8-3

Eunise 4-6-1

Eva 6-4-1

Evan 6-9-6

Eve 1-4-5

Evelyn 1-1-2

Fabian 2-4-6

Faith 1-7-8

Faye 6-4-1

Fergus 8-5-4

Filbert 5-4-9

Fiona 7-2-9

Flint 9-7-7

Flora 7-9-7

Florence 7-8-6

Floyd 6-2-8

Frances 6-6-3

Francesca 7-9-7

Francesco 3-9-3

Francine 6-1-7

Francis 1-6-7

Francoise 3-6-9

Frank 1-4-5

Fraser 6-7-4

Fred 5-1-6

Fredrick 5-6-2

Frieda 6-1-7

Fritz 9-7-7

Fulbert 8-4-3

Fuller 8-3-2

Gabriella 7-6-4

Gareth 6-8-5

Garret 6-9-6

Garth 1-8-9

Gary 1-5-6

Gavin 1-7-8

Gena 6-3-9

Geoffrey 7-8-6

George 7-5-3

Georgia 3-5-8

Georgina 3-1-4

Georgio 8-5-4

Gerald 6-5-2

Geraldine 2-1-3

Gerry 5-5-1

Gertrude 4-4-8

Gil 9-1-1

Gilbert 5-5-1

Giles 5-2-7

Gillian 1-9-1

Gina 1-3-4

Glen 5-6-2

Glenda 6-1-7

Glenn 5-2-7

Glenna 6-2-8

Gloria 7-1-8

Glynis 9-5-5

Glynn 7-2-9

Gordon 3-7-1

Grace 6-1-7

Graeme 2-2-4

Graham 2-1-3

Grant 1-5-6

Greg 5-5-1

Gregory 2-3-5

Greta 6-9-6

Gretta 6-2-8

Guido 9-2-2

Guiseppe 4-4-8

Gunther 8-4-3

Guri 3-7-1

Gus 3-8-2

Guy 3-5-8

Hailley 6-3-9

Haley 6-9-6

Hank 1-6-7

Hannah 2-8-1

Hans 1-5-6

Harley 6-9-6

Harmonia 8-8-7

Harold 7-6-4

Harriet 6-1-7

Harriette 2-3-5

Harrison 7-5-3

Harry 1-6-7

Hartley 6-2-8

Harvey 6-1-7

Harvie 6-3-9

Hazel 6-1-7

Heather 2-9-2

Hector 2-4-6

Heidi 5-3-8

Helen 1-7-8

Helene 6-7-4

Helga 6-9-6

Henry 5-2-7

Herb 5-1-6

Hilary 1-9-1

Hilda 1-6-7

Hilma 1-6-7

Holly 6-3-9

Howard 7-8-6

Hubbard 4-7-2

Hubert 8-3-2

Hugh 3-5-8

Humphrey 8-7-6

Hunter 8-6-5

Huntley 8-7-6

Ian 1-5-6

Ida 1-4-5

Inga 1-3-4

Ingrid 9-7-7

Irene 1-5-6

Iris 9-1-1

Irma 1-4-5

Irwin 9-1-1

Isaac 2-4-6

Isabel 6-6-3

Isadora 8-5-4

Isobel 2-6-8

Ivan 1-9-1

Ivy 9-2-2

Jabir 1-3-4

Jack 1-6-7

Jackie 6-6-3

Jackson 7-3-1

Jacob 7-6-4

Jacqueline 5-2-7

Jacquelyn 9-9-9

Jacques 9-4-4

Jade 6-5-2

Jafar 2-7-9

James 6-6-3

Jamie 6-5-2

Jana 2-6-8

Jane 6-6-3

Janet 6-8-5

Janice 6-9-6

Janine 6-2-8

Janus 4-7-2

Jaques 9-1-1

Jasmine 6-2-8

Jason 7-7-5

Jay 1-8-9

Jean 6-6-3

Jeaninne 2-7-9

Jeffrey 1-2-3

Jenna 6-2-8

Jennifer 1-8-9

Jenny 5-9-5

Jeremy 1-3-4

Jerome 7-5-3

Jerry 5-8-4

Jess 5-3-8

Jessa 6-3-9

Jessica 6-6-3

Jessie 1-3-4

Jill 9-7-7

Jim 9-5-5

Jimmy 9-7-7

Jin 9-6-6

Jiri 9-1-1

Joan 7-6-4

Joanna 8-2-1

Joanne 3-2-5

Jocelyn 2-1-3

Jodi 6-5-2

Jody 6-3-9

Joe 2-1-3

Joel 2-4-6

Joelle 7-7-5

Joey 2-8-1

Johanna 8-1-9

John 6-5-2

Johnathan 8-2-1

Johnny 6-8-5

Jolene 7-9-7

Jon 6-6-3

Jonah 7-5-3

Jonathan 8-3-2

Jonathon 4-3-7

Jordan 7-1-8

Jordana 8-1-9

Jory 6-8-5

Joseph 2-8-1

Josephine 7-4-2

Joshua 1-1-2

Josiah 7-1-8

Josie 2-2-4

Joy 6-8-5

Joyce 2-2-4

Juan 4-6-1

Judah 4-4-8

Judas 4-6-1

Jude 8-5-4

Judith 3-6-9

Judy 3-3-6

Julia 4-4-8

Julian 4-9-4

Juliana 5-9-5

Julias 4-5-9

Julie 8-4-3

Julien 8-9-8

June 8-6-5

Juno 9-6-6

Justin 3-9-3

Justine 8-9-8

Kaela 7-5-3

Kaleb 6-7-4

Kamal 2-9-2

Karen 6-7-4
Karl 1-5-6
Karla 2-5-7
Karolina 8-1-9
Katelyn 6-1-7
Kathleen 2-2-4
Kathryn 1-6-7
Katie 6-4-1
Katrina 2-9-2
Kay 1-9-1
Kayla 2-3-5
Keath 6-3-9
Keith 5-3-8
Kelly 5-6-2
Ken 5-7-3
Kendra 6-2-8
Kenneth 1-4-5
Kent 5-9-5
Kerry 5-9-5
Kevan 5-2-7
Kim 9-6-6
Kimberley 1-9-1
King 9-5-5
Kip 9-9-9
Kirby 9-2-2
Kirk 9-4-4
Kit 9-4-4
Kitty 9-4-4
Klaus 4-6-1

Kody 6-4-1
Konrad 7-2-9
Kory 6-9-6
Kristen 5-1-6
Kristi 9-5-5
Kristin 9-1-1
Kristy 9-3-3
Kurt 3-4-7
Kurtis 3-5-8
Kyla 1-3-4
Lance 6-2-8
Landon 7-8-6
Lane 6-8-5
Lara 2-3-5
Larisa 2-4-6
Larry 1-1-2
Lars 1-4-5
Laura 5-3-8
Laurel 9-6-6
Lauren 9-8-8
Laurence 5-2-7
Laurie 9-3-3
Lawrence 2-7-9
Layne 6-6-3
Lea 6-3-9
Leah 6-2-8
Leanne 2-4-6
Lee 1-3-4
Leigh 5-9-5

Lemuel 4-1-5
Lena 6-8-5
Lenora 3-8-2
Leo 2-3-5
Leona 3-8-2
Leonard 3-3-6
Leora 3-3-6
Leroy 2-1-3
Les 5-4-9
Leslie 1-7-8
Levi 5-7-3
Lew 5-8-4
Li 9-3-3
Lilly 9-7-7
Lily 9-4-4
Lin 9-8-8
Linda 1-3-4
Lindsay 1-2-3
Lindsey 5-2-7
Lisa 1-4-5
Liv 9-7-7
Lloyd 6-8-5
Logan 7-6-4
Lois 6-4-1
Lola 7-6-4
Lorea 3-3-6
Loreen 7-8-6
Lorelei 7-6-4
Lorenda 3-3-6

Loreta 3-5-8
Loretta 3-7-1
Lori 6-3-9
Lorna 7-8-6
Lorne 2-8-1
Lorraine 3-8-2
Lou 9-3-3
Louis 9-4-4
Louise 5-4-9
Luc 3-6-9
Lucas 4-7-2
Lucian 4-2-6
Lucie 8-6-5
Lucile 8-9-8
Lucille 8-3-2
Lucinda 4-6-1
Lucy 3-4-7
Luis 3-4-7
Lukas 4-6-1
Luke 8-5-4
Lydia 1-5-6
Lyle 5-4-9
Lynn 7-4-2
Lynne 5-2-7
Mabel 6-9-6
Madeleine 7-7-5
Madonna 8-9-8
Mae 6-4-1
Maggie 6-9-6

Mahalia 3-6-9

Mahara 3-3-6

Maia 2-4-6

Malcolm 7-8-6

Mallory 7-8-6

Malu 4-7-2

Manuel 9-3-3

Marcellus 9-5-5

Marco 7-7-5

Marcus 4-8-3

Marg 1-2-3

Margaret 7-4-2

Marge 6-2-8

Margo 7-2-9

Maria 2-4-6

Marian 2-9-2

Marianna 3-5-8

Marianne 7-5-3

Marie 6-4-1

Marilyn 1-1-2

Mario 7-4-2

Marisa 2-5-7

Marius 4-5-9

Marjorie 3-5-8

Mark 1-6-7

Marlene 2-3-5

Marlon 7-3-1

Marshall 2-1-3

Martha 2-5-7

Martin 1-2-3

Marvin 1-4-5

Mary 1-2-3

Mason 7-1-8

Mathew 6-1-7

Matilda 2-4-6

Matt 1-8-9

Matthew 6-3-9

Maud 4-8-3

Maureen 5-9-5

Maurice 9-7-7

Max 1-1-2

Maxine 6-6-3

May 1-2-3

Maya 2-2-4

Meaghan 7-6-4

Meara 7-4-2

Megan 6-7-4

Meghan 6-6-3

Mel 5-7-3

Melanie 2-3-5

Melinda 6-7-4

Melissa 6-9-6

Melody 2-9-2

Meredith 1-9-1

Merv 5-8-4

Michael 6-9-6

Michaela 7-9-7

Michelle 1-3-4

Mick 9-9-9	Nadine 6-5-2
Miguel 8-5-4	Nadir 1-9-1
Mike 5-6-2	Nan 1-1-2
Mildred 5-6-2	Nancy 1-2-3
Miles 5-8-4	Naomi 7-9-7
Millie 5-1-6	Natalia 3-1-4
Min 9-9-9	Natalie 7-1-8
Miri 9-4-4	Natasha 3-7-1
Miriam 1-8-9	Nathalie 7-9-7
Mitchell 5-5-1	Nathan 2-2-4
Mohammad 8-6-5	Nathaniel 7-5-3
Mohammed 3-6-9	Neal 6-8-5
Mohan 7-8-6	Ned 5-9-5
Moira 7-4-2	Neil 5-8-4
Molly 6-8-5	Nell 5-2-7
Mona 7-9-7	Nellie 1-2-3
Monica 7-3-1	Nelson 2-5-7
Monique 5-8-4	Neville 1-6-7
Monroe 8-9-8	Nicholas 7-2-9
Montana 8-7-6	Nick 9-1-1
Montgomery 8-2-1	Nicola 7-2-9
Morgan 7-7-5	Nicole 2-2-4
Morris 6-5-2	Nigel 5-6-2
Muhammad 5-6-2	Nikki 9-9-9
Murdock 9-4-4	Nils 9-9-9
Murial 4-7-2	Nina 1-1-2
Muriel 8-7-6	Noah 7-4-2
Murray 4-2-6	Noel 2-8-1
Myles 5-6-2	Nolan 7-4-2

Nora 7-5-3

Norbert 2-9-2

Noreen 7-1-8

Norma 7-9-7

Norman 7-5-3

Norton 3-3-6

Octavio 4-9-4

Ola 7-3-1

Olga 7-1-8

Olive 2-7-9

Oliver 2-7-9

Olivia 7-7-5

Omar 7-4-2

Oscar 7-4-2

Osvaldo 4-3-7

Otto 3-4-7

Owen 2-1-3

Pablo 7-3-1

Paige 6-5-2

Pamela 7-5-3

Pat 1-9-1

Patricia 2-3-5

Patsy 1-8-9

Paul 4-1-5

Paula 5-1-6

Pauline 9-6-6

Pearl 6-1-7

Peggy 5-1-6

Penelope 3-4-7

Penny 5-6-2

Percy 5-8-4

Perry 5-5-1

Peter 1-9-1

Petula 9-3-3

Phil 9-9-9

Philip 9-7-7

Philippe 5-5-1

Phillip 9-1-1

Phyllis 9-2-2

Pierre 1-7-8

Preston 2-6-8

Prudence 4-1-5

Quentin 8-2-1

Quincy 3-5-8

Quinn 3-9-3

Quon 9-4-4

Rachael 7-5-3

Rachel 6-5-2

Rae 6-9-6

Ralph 1-9-1

Ramon 7-9-7

Ramona 8-9-8

Randall 2-6-8

Randy 1-7-8

Raquel 9-2-2

Rasheda 7-4-2

Rashida 2-4-6

Ravi 1-4-5

Ray 1-7-8
Raymond 7-2-9
Raymund 4-2-6
Rebecca 2-8-1
Reece 6-3-9
Reg 5-7-3
Reid 5-4-9
Renata 7-7-5
Renee 6-5-2
Rex 5-6-2
Rhoda 7-3-1
Richard 1-6-7
Rick 9-5-5
Ricky 9-3-3
Riley 5-1-6
Rita 1-2-3
Robert 2-4-6
Roberta 3-4-7
Roberto 8-4-3
Robin 6-7-4
Robina 7-7-5
Robyn 6-5-2
Rock 6-5-2
Rod 6-4-1
Rodney 2-7-9
Roger 2-7-9
Rohana 8-4-3
Roland 7-3-1
Romeo 8-4-3

Ronald 7-3-1
Ronnie 2-1-3
Rory 6-7-4
Rosa 7-1-8
Rosalee 8-4-3
Rosalind 7-4-2
Rosaline 3-9-3
Rosanna 8-2-1
Rosanne 3-2-5
Rosaria 8-1-9
Roscoe 8-4-3
Rose 2-1-3
Rosemarie 8-5-4
Rosemary 3-3-6
Ross 6-2-8
Rossanne 3-3-6
Rowena 3-1-4
Roxanne 3-7-1
Roy 6-7-4
Royce 2-1-3
Ruben 8-7-6
Ruby 3-9-3
Rudy 3-2-5
Rupert 8-9-8
Russ 3-2-5
Russell 8-8-7
Ruth 3-1-4
Ryan 1-3-4
Sabrina 2-8-1

Salim 1-8-9
Sally 1-5-6
Sam 1-5-6
Samantha 3-2-5
Samara 3-5-8
Samson 7-2-9
Samuel 9-8-8
Sandra 2-1-3
Sandy 1-8-9
Sara 2-1-3
Sarah 2-9-2
Sasha 2-1-3
Saul 4-4-8
Scott 6-8-5
Sean 6-6-3
Sebastian 7-2-9
Serena 2-6-8
Shane 6-5-2
Sharon 7-5-3
Shaun 4-5-9
Shauna 5-5-1
Shawn 1-1-2
Shea 6-9-6
Sheena 2-5-7
Sheila 6-3-9
Shelagh 6-9-6
Sheldon 2-3-5
Shelley 1-4-5
Shen 5-5-1

Sherry 5-7-3
Shirley 5-1-6
Sid 9-5-5
Sidney 5-8-4
Sigrid 9-3-3
Simon 6-1-7
Simone 2-1-3
Sondra 7-1-8
Sonia 7-6-4
Sonja 7-7-5
Sonya 7-4-2
Sophia 7-7-5
Sophie 2-7-9
Spencer 1-7-8
Stacey 6-4-1
Stacie 6-6-3
Stacy 1-4-5
Stan 1-8-9
Stanley 6-9-6
Stavros 7-8-6
Stefan 6-5-2
Stella 6-9-6
Stephanie 2-5-7
Stephen 1-5-6
Steve 1-7-8
Stewart 6-1-7
Stuart 4-5-9
Sue 8-1-9
Sunny 3-9-3

Suria 4-1-5	Thomas 7-6-4
Susan 4-7-2	Tim 9-6-6
Susanna 5-3-8	Timothy 6-5-2
Susanne 9-3-3	Tina 1-7-8
Susie 8-2-1	Tobias 7-5-3
Suzanna 5-1-6	Todd 6-1-7
Sybil 9-4-4	Tom 6-6-3
Sydney 5-6-2	Tommy 6-8-5
Sylvia 1-6-7	Toni 6-7-4
Sylvie 5-6-2	Tony 6-5-2
Talia 2-5-7	Tracy 1-3-4
Tamara 3-6-9	Trent 5-9-5
Tammy 1-8-9	Trenton 2-5-7
Tara 2-2-4	Trevor 2-6-8
Tatiana 3-9-3	Tristan 1-1-2
Tatum 4-8-3	Troy 6-9-6
Tatyana 3-7-1	Truman 4-2-6
Taylor 7-3-1	Tyler 5-3-8
Ted 5-6-2	Tylor 6-3-9
Terence 6-1-7	Tyrone 2-5-7
Terra 6-2-8	Tyson 6-6-3
Terri 5-2-7	Unice 8-8-7
Terry 5-9-5	Uriel 8-3-2
Tess 5-4-9	Ursula 7-4-2
Tessa 6-4-1	Valerie 2-7-9
Thea 6-1-7	Vanessa 7-2-9
Thelma 6-8-5	Velma 6-2-8
Theodore 4-5-9	Vera 6-4-1
Theresa 2-2-4	Veronica 3-3-6

Vi 9-4-4
Victor 6-9-6
Victoria 7-9-7
Vince 5-3-8
Vincent 5-1-6
Violet 2-9-2
Virgil 9-5-5
Virginia 1-7-8
Vivian 1-4-5
Wade 6-9-6
Wallace 7-5-3
Walt 1-1-2
Walter 6-1-7
Wanda 2-5-7
Warren 6-1-7
Wayne 6-8-5
Wendy 5-3-8
Wesley 1-7-8
Whitney 5-9-5
Wilbur 3-1-4
Wilf 9-5-5
Will 9-2-2
William 1-6-7
Wilma 1-3-4
Wing 9-8-8
Winifred 5-2-7
Winnie 5-6-2
Woody 3-7-1
Yasmin 1-8-9

Yolanda 8-1-9
Yves 5-3-8
Yvonne 2-3-5
Zachary 2-8-1
Zahira 2-7-9

NAME ANALYSIS

The preceding eighty-one analyses have attemped to stimulate some interest in this radical and fascinating idea that your life could possibly have something to do with the name you have been given.

My study of the subject has indicated that this knowledge has been known and studied quite extensively in most ancient cultures, mostly by select groups or individuals and always in secret. They may have kept their study secret for several reasons: a) this knowledge was too radical for the general population; b) they feared being ridiculed or ostracized; 3) non-conformity with an established religion was considered heresy and invited persecution, etc.

As in all times, theories and ideas that are not approved by the mainstream forces, such as academia or the scientific community, find it difficult to be accepted. Unfortunately, this knowledge under the heading "numerology" has been relegated to the scrapheap of occultism.

In reality, this knowledge is not difficult to prove or to demonstrate. With an open mind, anyone can understand the principles involved. A complete name analysis is the best way of proving the point. Then if you wish to investigate further, there are profoundly revealing home study courses that are easy to follow. For a complete analysis of your life send the following information:

Full Legal Name
Gender (male or female)
Maiden Name
Name Mostly Used
Business Signature (please print)
Birthdate (Month, Day, Year)
Time of Birth (if near midnight)
Address (including Zip or Postal Code)
Phone Number
The analysis will be on a 60- or 90-minute
audio cassette tape.

Mail this information along with your fee
($65 US or $80 Canadian) to:
Clayne Conings,
123 N. Holdom Ave,
Burnaby, B.C. V5B 1K2
Canada.
Telephone: 604-299-2337

If you are interested in home study courses, the
first course offered through correspondence is $270
US or $300 Canadian. It includes eleven 100-minute
audio cassette tapes with easy to follow written material. This course gives detailed instructions for
working out people's names and the entire process of
analysis.

ABOUT THE AUTHOR

Clayne Conings admits to having no letters after his name but believes that the letters in his name have far greater significance. In his youthful idealism, he joined the Canadian Navy when he was seventeen to begin a 25-year career. Two days into boot camp, he realized that he had made a great mistake. At 19 he decided to become a famous actor. To this day, he still sings and dances his way through life but feels that nobody recognizes his talents. He teaches Scottish Country Dancing and plays the accordion.

At twenty-three, he changed his name and knew that he had discovered something that could revolutionize the way we all think. His early self-confidence was a product of his athletic prowess, which he can still be heard boasting about. From twenty-five to thirty-five years of age, while the new name forced him to establish some level of practicality in his life, he wasn't sure whether he was living in Heaven or Hell. For twelve years he worked in a small importing company and thanks his business colleague, Steve Webster, for giving him a chance and for putting up with him. In recent times he considers himself an unqualified master mechanic of the Volvo Penta marine engine in his old boat, particularly in taking the thing apart.

His wife, Cathrine, particularly, and his son Hugh have no small part in his success at this point in his life.

It was through the pioneering efforts of the late Alfred J. Parker that Clayne came to understand the profound principle contained in mathematics in relation to language and your name, and for thirty-two years this study has been his passion. His teaching of this work has been his commitment and his very reason for life.

SUMMARY

This book is an introduction to a principle that contains the whole meaning of your life, keeping in mind that your first name is only part of the whole picture. It is designed to capture your attention by appealing to your interest in yourself. The deeper meaning of this work is veiled within each of the eighty-one analyses. To those who know that personal change or transformation is an almost impossible task, this work will suggest or imply a profound truth. Years ago someone made the astute observation that "you could not change human nature," that you could see all the faults and character traits in a child that would reappear without change in that same child who had become an adult. Of course people can and do change their habits and attitudes, but these changes are not always significant enough to awaken to their true purpose in life. This book is an effort to reach out to those few who will further their interest in this study and see fit to recognize the importance of a balanced name. Only as we achieve individualization and a plane beyond the problematic states will we awaken the creative impulse.

For more information on Destynology:
http://www.destynology.com